Eel Pie Island Dharma

A hippie memoir/haibun

Chris Faiers

First Edition

Hidden Brook Press
www.HiddenBrookPress.com
writers@HiddenBrookPress.com

Eel Pie Island Dharma

Eel Pie Island Dharma: A hippie memoir/haibun
by Chris Faiers

Editor – Sylvia Hegge
Cover Design – Richard M. Grove
Layout and Design – Richard M. Grove
Cover Photograph of Bridge – Chris Faiers

First published as *Eel Pie Dharma: a memoir/haibun*,
Unfinished Monument Press, 1990

Typeset in Garamond

Printed and bound in USA

Library and Archives Canada Cataloguing in Publication

Faiers, Chris, 1948-
      Eel Pie Island Dharma : a hippie memoir/haibun / Chris Faiers.

ISBN 978-1-897475-92-8

      1. Faiers, Chris, 1948-. 2. Poets, Canadian (English)--20th century--Biography. 3. Haibun, Canadian (English). I. Title.

PS8561.A392Z53 2012   C811'.54   C2012-906436-X

Acknowledgements

Many thanks to friends who encouraged this memoir:

Poet Mark McCawley, who read the manuscript and encouraged me to publish it "as is",

Haijin John Hamley/snowflea, for writing the thoughtful introduction,

Fellow Eel Pie Island communard Weed, who posted it on his website, and who has let us include his own unique memoir of Eel Pie days in the addendum,

Eric Amann, godfather of Canadian haiku, who published my first haiku in 1967/68 in his seminal magazine *Haiku*,

Tai and Kim Grove, publishers of Hidden Brook Press. Tai has been advocating for this reprint for as long as we've been friends and poetry collaborators.

To my mother, Marianne, for giving me a lifelong love of literature.

Finally, to my longtime friend and editor, Sylvia Hegge, for patience and support.

Oops, and to Chase, my shih-tzu-on-steroids familiar, who kept me company through the final stages of preparation ... Wroooooooooooooof!

Eel Pie Island Dharma - a memoir / haibun

Introduction

I like books that open new worlds for me. This is one. It will take you on a tour of the weird and wonderful world of hippies—not as seen by an outsider or imagined by us ordinary people, but as remembered by a genuine draft-resisting, love-making, pot-smoking 1960s hippie.

Things like that couldn't happen today. The world has changed. I remember going to a love-in on a California beach in 1966, where the security was provided by the Hells Angels and everything went swimmingly. Even with the brutality of the Vietnam War in the background, in some ways our society was more innocent then.

The literary form of this memoir is haibun—prose narrative mixed with haiku—a form that dates back to the accounts of the first haiku master Matsuo Bashō of his long journeys on foot in Japan in the late 1600s. His *The Narrow Road to the Deep North and Other Travel Sketches* still makes exemplary reading. Chris Faiers' *Eel Pie Dharma*, first published in 1990, is one of the early applications of haibun in the English language.

Chris, an acknowledged pioneer of English-language haiku, has been writing haiku for over forty-four years and has published them by the hundreds. So, what are they like? Here are two examples from this book:

Awakening
to a naked man
with a peeled egg

England
sheep grazing
among gravestones

Players of the Oriental board game Go have a proverb: "If a move is not necessary, it is bad." Chris writes haiku like that. With a good eye for telling detail, and leaving everything else out, and never stooping to cleverness, he gives you simple unadorned kernels of what he saw or felt. You can take them or leave them.

In many ways, this little book gives us much to think about. But you don't need to think about it, you can just jump in and let Chris take you for a ride.

John Hamley/snowflea

Preface from the author

Writing *Eel Pie Dharma*:
Haibun as Memoir, Historical Document and Sacred Biography

Chris Faiers/cricket

I wrote *Eel Pie Dharma: a memoir/haibun* in the fall of 1988. I had quit my job as a desk clerk at Toronto Public Library, and was living on unemployment insurance. I self-published it in 1990 with Unfinished Monument Press. About a decade ago my webmaster, Weed, put it online.

EPD is the story of my adventures from the summer of 1969, when I dodged the draft for the Vietnam War, until 1972, when I returned to Canada, land of my birth. During much of those three years I lived in an abandoned hotel in Twickenham, England with a band of hippie squatters, the Eel Pie Island Commune.

For two decades I had told and retold stories of those heady times. After almost two decades, I decided it was crucial to capture these adventures while the memories remained fresh. So I quit the library, with plans to write my debut novel, a bildungsroman perhaps, like James Joyce's *A Portrait of the Artist as a Young Man*. Or more likely a freeform memoir like one of Jack Kerouac's biographical tales of being *On the Road* as a wandering beatnik Dharma Bum.

I set a strict daily schedule, and every afternoon I would go for a long hike to encourage the endorphin flow before settling at my typewriter for a minimum of one hour of productive writing.

An "accidental" haibun

There was no initial intention to write a haibun. I drew up a list of the most memorable events, and then began writing short passages about each. The first chapter, A Psychedelic Basho, contained a lot of haiku. I am fortunate to be among the early English language haiku poets, and this first chapter chronicles my introduction to a lifetime of writing haiku.

Other passages also contained haiku, and I found remembering poems I had written keyed profound memories of events. I was in the process of creating both a haibun as well as a memoir, with these two genres interacting and stimulating the creative process. However, these passages were still intended to be notes for a later fleshing out into full-fledged chapters in a traditional novel.

In January of 1989 I sold my tiny house in east end Toronto and moved to the old mining hamlet of Cordova Mines. I bought a rambling and ramshackle century farmhouse, and spent that summer fixing it up as best as possible. In the winter I renewed my task of writing *EPD*, sitting upstairs every night peering through dusty windows at the rundown church across the way while basking in the dull glow of the solitary Cordova streetlight.

I decided to copytype a cleaner version of the manuscript over the winter months. I had revised many of the 28 "chapters" that summer, adding haiku to the chapters which lacked them. In my subconscious I was creating a haibun, although I hadn't yet consciously reached this conclusion.

Poet Mark McCawley arranged a Canada Council reading for me for Valentine's Day 1990. I stayed with Mark and his wife for a week in Edmonton, where they were friendly and supportive hosts. One night I shyly mentioned the manuscript to Mark. The next morning Mark gave an enthusiastic response to the work-in-progress. But Mark added a twist, "Publish it as it is. It reads well and it's concise."

And so *EPD* greeted the world as a 58 page, cirlox bound, 8 ½ by 11 inch photocopied book published by my small literary press, Unfinished Monument. Over two decades later I still feel indebted to Mark for encouraging me to just go ahead and publish the manuscript "as is".

The first copies were published with the subtitle "a memoir/novella". Although there are now hundreds of thousands of entries for haibun on Google searches, in 1990 there were only two previous Canadian haibun of which I was aware.

Two earlier Canadian haibun

Jack Cain published his evocative short haibun, *Paris*, in 1964. It is available online at: http://thehaikufoundation.org/diglib/ch1.pdf pages 12 – 15 of *up against the window: contemporary haibun Volume 1* edited by Jim Kacian and Bruce Ross.

Rod Willmot published the lyrically beautiful *The Ribs of Dragonfly* with Black Moss Press in 1984. So to the best of my knowledge, *EPD* was the third Canadian haibun and only the second published Canadian haibun of book length (again, not counting the incredible beat generation books by Jack Kerouac). I have the vaguest memory of telling Rod I was quitting my library job to write fulltime, as Rod had inscribed my copy of *TROD* with "Chris – welcome to vagabondage!"

In retrospect I wonder why we haijin members of Haiku Canada were hesitant to publish haibun. Perhaps we were daunted at presenting our work for comparison with ancient masters like Basho. For decades most haiku poets remained content to publish small chapbooks of haiku, and without the prose framework, the context of these individual haiku was missing. No matter how evocative the poems, without a supporting prose structure, the haiku remained orphaned slices of momentary awareness.

Surprise use as online resource

It's been over two decades since I first published *EPD*. Fellow communard from Eel Pie Island days, Weed (once Chris Whitehouse), encouraged me to let him post it online about a decade ago. According to Weed, *EPD* has since been accessed by tens of thousands of readers. An unanticipated result of *EPD*'s availability on the web has been its establishment as an historical document. *EPD* has been quoted in 2 recent rock histories: *Won't Get Fooled Again* and *Eel Pie Island*.

Rock histories

British novelist Hari Kunzru also used *EPD* as an historical resource for his novel *My Revolutions*. Kunzru credits the chapter on the 144 Piccadilly Squat for background insight into the mindset of a young revolutionary member of Britain's Angry Brigades.
http://www.harikunzru.com/archive/novels/recolutions

U.K.'s All Out Productions also interviewed me as a resource for a 2007 BBC Radio 4 documentary on the Thames Valley Music Scene, in which the Eel Pie Hotel Ballroom provided a nurturing venue for the early days of The Stones and many other groups.

Sacred biography

Victoria Urubshurow, in *The Complete Idiot's Guide to: The Life of Buddha*, uses the phrase "sacred biography". I love her term "sacred biography", for this is what all true haibun are. There have been periods in my life when I've 'lost myself', forgotten the highest levels of consciousness I have experienced and described in several chapters of *Eel Pie Dharma*: meditating with a Buddhist monk in the London monastery, or having Swami A. C. Bhaktivedanta, the founder of the Hare Krishnas, look me in the eyes and tell how he remembers working with me for the betterment of mankind in previous incarnations. This aspect of haibun has been the most personally beneficial for me, although when I re-read *EPD* every few years I always reflect on the Grateful Dead's famous lyrics, "what a long strange trip it's been!"

Marmora, Ontario
May 15, 2011

BBC Radio 4.
→ Thames Valley Music Scene.

Chapter 1

A Psychedelic Basho

At community college I began writing bad poetry around 1967. When I realized that I was not cut out to be a science student, I immersed myself in arts courses and declared myself a poet. Some poems submitted to the student magazine reminded the editor of haiku. Having never heard of haiku, I didn't know what to make of the comment, but browsing through a literary magazine I found a classified ad offering copies of *Haiku* magazine from a Toronto address.

Haiku duly arrived, and I fell in love with the haiku form. The similarity between haiku and the brief poems I had been attempting was obvious, and soon I was submitting haiku to the editor of *Haiku*, Dr. Eric Amann.

After initial rejections I was thrilled when Eric Amann accepted several haiku for his magazine. Encouraged, I began to devote myself to writing haiku. Basho, the wandering haiku poet/priest of medieval Japan, was added to my role models. The lonely life of a commuting college student in Florida presented a few of my early poems:

Christmas vacation
tame ducks starving
by the campus lake

Rain
gray doves
strung on a wire

Light breeze
striding across campus
a thin professor

Almost from the beginning of my student days I had been fighting an appeals battle with the draft board. Unfortunately I had registered in Georgia, just before our family moved back to Florida. In retrospect, and after corresponding with former classmates many years later, I believe that I was an easy target for the Atlanta draft board. Living out of the state, drafting me wouldn't stir up any local antagonisms, and the fact that I was also a resident alien (as a Canadian citizen by birth) probably didn't help my cause. Ongoing struggles to keep my student status caused me to intensely question the Vietnam War, and I was living day-to-day with the life-and-death questions of duty to country versus participation in an unethical war. This personal turmoil provided a fertile ground for writing haiku poems. Often I had insomnia, and I would think back over my life. A family vacation in the Blue Ridge Mountains provided:

Cavern pool
tourists watching
blind fish

Memories of a far off Halloween in Canada when I was five years old inspired:

Halloween
a young boy
in a skeleton suit

Some days I would escape to the beach after class:

Lobster antennas
waving from the twin caves
of a cement block

Blue sea
bobbing red and white
lobster trap buoy

Summer moonlight
rotting on our roof
starfish

As I became more and more disillusioned with the Vietnam War, I
began to hang around with the other radicals and longhairs on the
campus. Miami was, and is, a very reactionary city, and psychedelia,
which had flowered in California in 1966, was just reaching Miami in
1968. I was one of the first longhairs on campus, and the second guy
on Key Biscayne to grow long hair. The centre for the slowly evolving
hippie community in Miami was Coconut Grove, an artistic haven
located around the Dinner Key docks and the adjacent waterfront park:

Bay wind blowing
Coconut Grove sailboats
tinkling rigging

First green appearing
buds on the new stake hedge
and chameleons

The flower
of this old tree
a treehouse

At the peak of the Vietnam War, in June 1969, I received three draft
notices in a week. It was time to leave. I flew from Miami to Nassau:

Mounted sailfish
lining the walls
of Nassau airport

From Nassau I caught a flight to Luxemburg, and then I caught a train
from Brussels to London:

Luxemburg
black paint on pink brick
U. ☂ A.

I lived with my cousin and his wife on the outskirts of London for several months. It wasn't a comfortable arrangement for any of us. I continued writing my haiku, always carrying a notebook with me in a tote bag. One of my first visits was to Piccadilly Circus, where the traffic island in the centre of the world's busiest intersection had become an international hippie rendezvous under the statue of Cupid. The day I visited Piccadilly there was a bust for hash smoking. A bobby was about to arrest me when he spied my London guide book, and he let me go:

Piccadilly Circus
Cupid's fountain spraying
hippies

By now I had a large collection of haiku, many of them published in *Haiku* and numerous other small haiku journals which had sprung up in the United States. I spent many days visiting Kew Gardens, and after one afternoon of meditation, I explored a side road on my way back to Kew Station. I found a little printing company, and somehow got the courage to go in.

"I'd like to publish a collection of my poems," I shyly told the balding, potbellied printer. Despite my hippie appearance, my American accent tipped him that I might have money, and he got me to show him what I wanted.

When he saw my Luxemburg poem with the swastika, he wanted to know if I was a fascist. I convinced him that I wasn't a fascist, only a poet, and he agreed to print my poetry in little booklets for £50 for 500 copies.

A week later I went back and picked up the box of my first chapbook, *Cricket Formations*. I lugged the booklets down the hill to the post office in the hamlet of Kew, and spent the afternoon mailing them all over the world.

Chapter 2

144 Piccadilly Squat

L'Auberge Cafe
ceramic Thames winds
past teacups

A concert in Hyde Park by the Edgar Broughton Band lured us downtown London. A group from L'Auberge took the tube to Hyde Park, where we lolled in the patchy grass through the concert. I remember everyone doodling all over my white turtleneck with coloured marker pens – it was a great excuse to roll around and get female attention and enjoy the camaraderie. The band finished with its trademark shout-along finale exorcism of "Out Demons, Out!" High from all the excitement we poured through the downtown streets, and three of us decided to take a stroll past the big squat that was being sensationalized in the newspapers.

144 Piccadilly was a huge, decaying stone building in the heart of the business district. Carefully we crossed the board planks laid across the moat-like no man's land. Like crossing the drawbridge into a decrepit urban castle. We had only planned to visit but we were so immediately accepted as kindred spirits that we just hung in. In one of the huge rooms upstairs a "war council" was being held. Many of the leaders were French students from the 1968 demonstrations in Paris. We huddled in a corner and basked in the excitement and dusty funkiness of it all.

We ended up in a little room with a couple in a sleeping-bag trying to make uncomfortable love:

Sleeping bag
stuffed, squirming
on bare boards

I went for a recon stroll and ended up on guard duty with a greaser. By now I realized that most of the original squatters had left and had been replaced by a few English "Hell's Angels", greasers (sort of understudy Angels), and a few other hippies and dossers like the couple in the sleeping bag. The front yard of 144 remained no man's land. Occasionally a few Angels would foray into the yard for a skirmish. A line of bobbies separated us from a howling mob of skinheads in Green Park across the street. The yowling, aggro skinheads reminded me of the orcs in *Lord of the Rings*. Our ammunition was rubber balls, most of which had been pumped full of water from hypodermic syringes – these were the waning days of legal junkiedom in the UK. Thousands of these toy balls had been stored in the basement. The greaser and I shared a turret-like window, peering into the dimming light at the bobbies and the taunting army of skinheads. "Watch me nail that bobby!" the greaser bragged, and he bopped one of Britain's finest in the helmet. My turn on guard. Three or four stories below us a limo was winding its way passed the entrenched riot. I thought 'I'll teach you to arrogantly drive through a battle zone like fucking tourists' and threw a ball. I don't know if I dented the roof, but the car sped away, and in that moment I felt the thrill and danger of commitment. Certainly I was now going to get a year or two in a British cell for throwing that ball. For me, the revolution was here.

We stayed a day or so. Tiring of the diet of countercultural soup and the building paranoia of an impending police raid, we decided to try and get out. We weren't sure if we would be allowed to leave by the other squatters, and I was sure that if we were, I was going to be arrested on damning evidence taken by a police photographer. Incredible tension was in the air when we got downstars to the main hallway. Everyone was preparing for an all-out assault by the police.

Angels and greasers were running round with balls and clubs and wrapping leather belts around their wrists. The biggest, meanest, ugliest renegade skinhead I had ever seen was standing guard by the front door with a great big club. Nobody tried to stop us, or even seemed to mind that we were leaving the impending battle scene. Perhaps they thought we would be beaten by the police anyway. We did. We crossed carefully back over the planks of no man's land towards the waiting line of blue. The worst was about to come - beaten silly on a London street, then beaten again at the police station, and finally five years in a cell. "Just a couple of dossers," one of the cops sneered as we reached the end of the planks. Amazed, we just kept walking. Freedom! We couldn't believe it. Later the police raided. We had walked out hours before the siege ended.

Chapter 3

The Day We (Sort Of)
Met George Harrison

It was late summer. A bunch of L'Auberge regulars decided to take a Sunday trek to see George Harrison, who was rumoured to be living in a little village named Esher. We hopped on the double-decker bus in Richmond, and after an hour or so of riding we arrived in Esher. The ten of us were a scraggly lot, all would-be hippies trying to grow our hair long, the girls dressed in shawls and long skirts and granny boots.

Our goals were the standard ones in 1969 - California Jon, Canadian Peter and a couple of other guitarists had made a tape, and wanted Harrison's opinion of it. I had a copy of my just printed haiku chapbook, *Cricket Formations*, and I hoped to get up enough nerve to present my poems to my idol. And of course we all wanted to meet a real live Beatle!

Harrison was my favourite Beatle, largely because he was the one closest to me in physical appearance, with his craggy face and dark hair. I had modeled my haircut and clothes on Harrison for some time. I also thought he was the most interesting Beatle because of his enthusiasm for Eastern mysticism.

Someone had gotten good directions, for we actually found Harrison's house without a lot of trouble. Located in a very staid, upper- middle-class suburban neighbourhood, the house stood out like a psychedelic advertisement. A high fence bordered the large lot, and the house was painted a myriad of colours, like something out of the movie *Yellow Submarine*. We were all entranced to be setting foot in a sacred preserve of Beatledom, and after knocking on the door and receiving no answer, we boldly began surveying the premises.

"MICK & MARIANNE WUZ HERE!" was spray painted on the front wall, and this further consecrated the property. Our rock heroes actually lived here, visited with each other, slept together, and had probably done these wild paintings on acid trips like our own. We were all strengthened in our faith as true believers in hippiedom.

Some of the group camped by the front door, and the guitar players started scratching on their ubiquitous instruments. I wandered around, and found a pair of George's jeans hanging on a clothesline. For a fleeting moment I was tempted to steal them, to see if my hero's jeans would fit.

Manicured lawn
would-be hippies wait
for a Beatle

A touch of the Beatles' famous ironic humour was present in a large wooden cross leaning against the back fence. I even had the nerve to peek in the draped windows. On the window ledge of one room was a collection of seashells. Miracle of miracles - there was even an apple tree - how appropriate for the founders of Apple records. If there was a heaven on earth, this was it for Beatle fans.

Seashell lined window
apples rotting in the yard
suburban fences

I rejoined the group on the front lawn, and soon a mini car came scooting up the drive, quickly followed by a luxury sedan. The driver of the mini got out, and a not-very-pleased looking George Martin confronted us. He wanted to know what we were doing, and while we all sat there stunned, George and Patti Harrison disembarked from the sedan. George wasn't really very prepossessing at all, but Patti was a vision of beauty, a psychedelic queen who smiled on us and calmed down the two very aggravated Georges. She knew that we were harmless fans come to honour Beatledom, and while she smiled her guileless smile, we felt like we were in the presence of a divine goddess from another reality. Canadian Peter recovered first, and awkwardly handed George Harrison the tape, mumbling something. I followed suit, even more awkwardly giving George my thin booklet, and saying I hoped he would enjoy it.

An invitation inside was not forthcoming, although I believe Patti wanted to ask us in. We were so enthralled at meeting George and Patti, awkward as all involved had been, that we decamped and blissfully headed back in the dusk for the bus to Richmond.

Several weeks later, a few members of the entourage went back to pick up the tape. Apparently a record contract wasn't immediately offered, but Canadian Peter did have some good news for me, "George Harrison told me to tell you that he really liked your poetry." I was thrilled, even though I now realized that Harrison was a mere, awkward mortal, and I was no longer in his thrall. As a postscript, I note that George Harrison's first solo album, *All Things Must Pass*, had the lyrics printed on the sleeve like poems. I like to fantasize that maybe my booklet had some subtle influence, but that's wild hope and speculation ...

Chapter 4
The Isle of Wight Concert

After a couple of months of unpleasant co-existence, my cousin asked me to leave, immediately. I was flung out with nowhere to go in a strange country. I wandered around the suburban village of Kingston upon Thames for the evening, and finally made a camp out of a suitcase and towels in a vacant lot:

**Making camp
in a vacant lot
with outcast cats**

I survived the night, and the next day I ran into Martha at L'Auberge. Martha's parents were going to Ibiza for a week with her younger sister. Supposedly it was ok for a few of us to stay with Martha for company. Soon the house was full of hippie crashers. Martha's sometimes boyfriend Canadian Peter, family friend Mark Valiant, myself and assorted L'Auberge regulars took advantage of the Holmes' hospitality.

The week flew by in a stoned haze. One night a group of the Richmond dossers dropped acid. One of them stabbed at the kitchen table with a knife for hours. So much for peace and love. A group of us trooped out into nearby Richmond Park, and cavorted in the moonlight all night.

Another memory of that week is of being awakened on the sofa by

Canadian Pete sticking a huge joint in my mouth. I toked and then fell back asleep against the expensive stereo cabinet.

The day the Holmes were due to return Mark organised frenzied work teams. We vacuumed the whole house, scrubbed floors, cleaned out the roach-filled ashtrays, did the dishes. For a final touch I decided to have a bath. While the bath was running, I continued with the massive clean-up. I was working in the livingroom when someone noticed a strange bubble forming on the ceiling. It was like something out of a horror movie, and in our permanently stoned state we first thought it was a group hallucination. And then the hallucinatory bubble began to drip. Panicked, I remembered my bath filling upstairs. I rushed up to find a foot or two of water flooding the bathroom.

I cut off the faucets, and somebody tried to lance the huge boil growing just above the dining table.

At this juncture the Holmes arrived! All our hours of cleaning were destroyed by my forgetfulness. In an amazingly controlled voice Mr. Holmes ordered me out of his house. I limped off to Richmond Park, where I sat on the side of a hill overlooking a field and cursed my stupidity.

In this depressed state I had nowhere to go, no one to turn to. I remembered hearing about a giant rock festival featuring Bob Dylan which was going to be held soon on the Isle of Wight. Having nothing better to do, I started walking in the general direction of Southampton, the crossing point for the Isle. I only made it to the edge of Richmond by dark. A lot of other young people were heading for the Isle of Wight, and I hooked up with a group of guys and walked with them for a mile or so before we decided to kip down for the night beside the Thames. We washed down sandwiches with a shared bottle of soda, and soon the fog and the darkness surrounded us. I woke up early in the morning. Through the dawn mist a pair of Thames swans swam majestically towards us; an omen for a better day:

Through dawn mist
floating
pair of Thames swans

Someone gave me a lift to Southampton, which wasn't really that far away. I only had a few pounds left in a post office bank account, and I withdrew my last worldly assets. I spent part of the day mooning around Southampton, trying to track down a girl I had met at the Plumpton Festival. Her parents must have got wind of her plans, or else she had lost interest in me, because I wasn't able to arrange a meeting by phone. So I crossed over to the Isle of Wight on one of the giant tourist ferries.

The whole ferry was crowded with young people on their way to the concert. Hippies, students, and would-be hippies like myself trying to grow their hair. When the ferry docked, I joined the long trail of hikers winding towards the concert site. Along the way locals had set up lemonade stands in the British tradition of combining shopkeeper capitalism and hospitality.

I fell in with two girls and another guy. When we reached the muddy concert site, it looked like a refugee camp. Thousands and thousands of young people were camping in open fields. This was just after the Woodstock Festival took place in New York State, and apparently there were more people at the Isle of Wight Festival than there were at Woodstock. However, as Woodstock took place in the United States, and was thus more important to the growing anti-Vietnam peace movement, Woodstock has gone down in history as the seminal and most important rock concert of the period. But it also happened, on a possibly larger scale, in the beautiful fields among the dramatic hills of the Isle of Wight.

We spent hours helping the girls raise their tent. Exhausted from the excitement and the trek, we curled up inside. The girl I was paired with rubbed against me most of the night, but she wouldn't do much more than that. We probably both found the other only marginally attractive, and I found the experience frustrating.

The next day I wandered off on my own into the huge crowd, and I soon found a welcome place in an earthen hut which housed a whole troupe of early arrivals. Rhino was one of the leaders. He was a rough looking but kindhearted guy, and there was also a gorgeous blonde heroin addict from Scandinavia. For some reason she liked me, and when I told her I was a writer and journalist, she was fascinated. All night we sat round a roaring campfire, telling our life stories and hopes and dreams:

Talked all night
ashes at dawn
girls asleep

The next night was the feature of the festival, Bob Dylan. I sat at the back of the hundreds of thousands of kids, and Dylan was just a doll-like figure hundreds of yards away, whose music barely reached me.

Crowds, dope, sleeping in the open air, smoke in our tangled hair. Sexual frustration, still. Weaving back in a queue of bodies miles long, past the lemonade stands to the ferry. Back to Southampton, where I again hooked up with the gorgeous heroin addict, who bragged that she was heading to New York, because it had the best smack in the world. We all piled into a van headed for London, and somehow I was in. I had survived some rite of passage, and the ten of us crowded in the back of the van sang and banged time on the tinny walls all the way back to Richmond. My beautiful heroin addict got out first, and I never saw her again.

Chapter 5
Bedsitters & Jools

I was on my own on the streets of Richmond. I couldn't sleep on the floors of the other L'Auberge habitues' crashpads forever, so I checked the classifieds and found a bedsitter near Kew Gardens.

A bedsitting room is just as cramped and depressing as it sounds. It's just a back bedroom, usually, with a hotplate for cooking meals. A workingperson's or student's cell. The landlady reluctantly let me rent her room for some exorbitant amount, and then laid down the house rules - and definitely no guests! On my first night several L'Auberge regulars needed a place to sleep, so I let them crash on my floor. How could I refuse after taking advantage of so many other people's hospitality?

The landlady was properly horrified when she knocked on my door late the next morning, and saw a roomful of sleeping hippies. I was given a very stern warning never to let anyone stay over again, which rule I promptly broke the next night when again a number of people didn't feel like sleeping in the park. So I was out.

Danny had just rented a bedsitter across the Richmond Bridge, and I willingly accepted an invitation to crash on his floor. Every dosser in the Richmond area made the scene, and we smoked hash and talked long into the night. I was curled up on the floor with Sophie. I knew she was some celebrity's daughter on the Richmond rock scene. We were both very stoned, and probably a lot more naive than we let on. I was still a virgin, and we just necked a bit and then fell asleep.

Bedsitter floor
dusty, curled
schoolkids

The next morning Danny left early for some labouring job, and I
slowly raised my drowsy body off the floor. A late riser as always,
finally there were only two of us left. Jools was a cute blonde girl I
had noticed looking at me often through the hash haze of the night
before. Even in my inexperience I realized that she was interested in
more than just talking to me. I can't remember all our conversations,
but I was full of poetry and romance, and she ate it up. I had never
made love before, and here was this nubile woman of sixteen, quite
experienced in sex and ready to have a go. I was too nervous and
egotistical to tell her that I was a virgin, and I really didn't have a clue
about what to do. We climbed onto Danny's bed, and she climbed on
top of me. She guided me into her sweet little pussy, and bim/bam in
less than a couple of minutes I wasn't a virgin

I wanted to have another go a little later when we woke up again.
Feeling cocky now that I was an experienced man, I climbed on top of
her, but her pussy wasn't lubricated, and I had to stop. Jools decided
to have a shower, and she wrapped herself in Danny's curtain so she
could go down the hall to the shared washroom. Sure enough, just as
she returned a knock came at the door, and another shocked landlady
was confronted with two semi-naked hippies. Of course Danny got
turfed out of his bedsitter that night.

small wet blonde
wrapped in a curtain

Chapter 6
Meeting Eel Pie

**"Out of college, money spent
see no future, pay no rent
all the money's gone
no place to go ..."**
Abbey Road, The Beatles

I nervously wandered off the curving streets of Richmond into the offices of the local newspaper to ask for a job. I was surprised when I was taken seriously. As a test assignment, the editor told me that a group of hippies had started a commune in an abandoned hotel in Twickenham, the next village along the Thames. The directions were fascinating - the hotel was called Eel Pie Island Hotel, and it really was on a little island in the middle of the Thames.

I caught the double-decker bus to Twickenham, and quickly found the arched footbridge which led to Eel Pie Island. It was about two hundred feet across the little bridge, with a beautiful view of the Thames. When I had reached the island I felt I had entered a special place. A footpath lined with neat little cottages wound through the centre of the island. There was no missing the old hotel at the end of the footpath. It was derelict, and I just walked in where the grand front entrance had once been.

Without any problems I quickly located the founder of the commune. Cliff was an artist/cartoonist and an anarchist. He was living with his

American girlfriend, Ame, in a large room on the second floor of the hotel. Cliff was a big bear of a man by English standards. He had long, strawlike brown hair and an unkempt beard. With his granny glasses he looked like a professor gone bad. Ame was an All-American girl - fresh-faced and clean limbed with glasses - a professor's wife gone bad.

Cliff's easel and layout table and supplies spilled over one half of their large room, and in the other half was a big old mattress on the floor covered with quilts and blankets. The scene was artsy and cozy and there was the musty smell of Thames dampness pervading.

It looked like an enticing way to live, very bohemian and independent and countercultural. As I introduced myself to begin the interview, I was compelled to say, "I'm really a poet, not a reporter."

"What kind of poetry?" Cliff wanted to know. "Mostly haiku poetry, it's a Japanese style," and I dug into my dolly bag to give them a copy of *Cricket Formations.*

"We want to build a commune of artists, especially politically conscious artists," Cliff explained. "Why don't you pick out a room to use as a study and you could live here as part of the commune. Only a couple of people have moved in so far. You'd have your pick of rooms."

This was too good an offer to resist. I dashed around the hollow building. Too Much! There were no flats available in the Greater London area. I had been turfed out of two bedsitters in a week, and here I was being offered a room of my own in this picturesque setting. Thoughts of the interview were forgotten. I was a poet again.

EEL PIE ISLAND

At first there were only a handful
of hippies in the derelict hotel
and I got a room
instead of a story
when I said I'm really a poet
not a reporter

Two years of my life
sleepstoned
hiding from the clammy Thames fog
only our black and brown hashish
smoke holding up the crumbling walls

It's all so trite ten years later
so far out and away
from the foggy decay
of spunksoaked mattresses

Dougie, Crippled Eddie, Lorna
Scotch John, Seamus
Angie - Dominic
Where are you now
as the world discos towards 1984
to lift my head off the floor
hand me a fuming chillum
to kiss me tonight

Chapter 7
Eel Piers

The old hotel rapidly filled with dossers, hippies, runaway schoolkids, drug dealers, petty thieves, heroin addicts, artists, poets, bikers, American hippie tourists, au pair girls, and Zen philosophers from all over the world.

Hundreds of mostly young people called the hotel home for at least a part of its final years as "The Eel Pie Commune".

I moved in with my buddy California Jon, and two of the L'Auberge regulars, Lisa and Lorna. Jon was one of the hippie tourists, and when the summer ended he returned to California. He did come back the next summer, but things weren't as magical as they had been in the summer of 1969.

Gavin was another early resident. He had long black hair and a thick beard, and I looked up to him at first as a role model. He was from a small English town, where he had tired of being the town freak, and had come to the big city to find kindred spirits. Gavin was into a garbled form of Zen, and I wrote the following haiku with him in mind:

After cold midnight
scraping burnt commune rice pot
on the lawn for birds

Another L'Auberge habitue who moved in was Lisa, who claimed to be related to Jimmy Page, the leader of the band Led Zeppelin. She shared a room with Lorna, and the two of them became hash dealers. They were perfectly suited to this occupation. It gave them an opportunity to meet lots of horny guys, and the lure of sexual favours, whether delivered or not, gave them a steady supply of customers wandering over the bridge.

Lorna got more and more into non-stop sex and drugs, and eventually she drifted into heroin addiction. I heard she died from an overdose about 1971. Lisa paired up with another L'Auberger, Roger, a big tough-looking guy with a Fu Manchu moustache who acted as her protector.

Thomas was another early resident. He was pals with Mark and Andrea. All three had artistic pretensions, and were into street theatre/psychodramatic activities. They were mostly annoying. My strongest memory of Thomas is of a tall gangly guy with a burr haircut on a small head. Thomas was what we called a power tripper. He liked to be an authority figure, although most of us just ignored him as a nuisance, but part of the ambience of Eel Pie.

Dealer Jim was an American black who had been touring the world. He was from the streets of the American southwest, and he couldn't believe the reality of Europe in the late 60s. Nobody called him "nigger" or "boy", even behind his back, although some people were a little prejudiced. Dealer Jim was the prototype of the crack dealers of the late 1980s. He was tough, streetwise, and muscular with a short cropped haircut, over which he often wore a black porkpie hat. He had scored a large amount of black hash in Morocco, and he carried a huge lump of it around with him everywhere.

Thomas didn't like Dealer Jim, perhaps due to racism, or more likely Dealer Jim had such a strong personality. One morning I awoke to a strange thumping sound, ending in a crash. I ran downstairs to the second floor, and found a throng standing around the landing leading to the ground level. At the bottom of the stairs sprawled Thomas, who had insulted Dealer Jim. Dealer Jim had replied in the universal language of the streets, for which he needed no training in street theatre dynamics. He had flung Thomas from the top to the bottom of the stairs. Thomas was much more subdued in the weeks that followed, and eventually wandered off to pester the residents of some hipper scene. Dealer Jim eventually made his way back to the US, with a wad of money made in the pubs and cafes of London.

Chapter 8
More Eel Piers

The crumbling hotel, where the Rolling Stones had played some of their first gigs, attracted more and more people. Prophet Chris was a bearded ex-psychology student from a major English university. He was in his late twenties, which at the time seemed old, especially as his roommate was Sean, an immature nineteen-year-old from the L'Auberge scene.

Two Scandinavian women in their early twenties joined us. They had been "au pair girls", a euphemism for domestic slaves. They had tired of working for demanding upper-class Brits and had run away from their assignments to the hotel. Heloise was dark and plumpish, and she spent a lot of time sewing her clothes and those of her friend Britt. Britt was blonde and thin and quite attractive.

Eventually the immigration authorities tracked them down, and to avoid deportation they decided to marry two of the Eel Pie men. We had a true hippie wedding, with a motley crew of twenty-five or so Eel Piers present at the registry office for a double wedding. We were all stoned as usual, and I ran out to an off-licence and bought some bottles of cheap wine.

One of the American hippie tourists, Margaret, took up housekeeping with Don, who was rumoured to have been a semi-pro soccer player. They spent most of their days in bed, although Don took to going to the local library, where he spent hours pouring over philosophy texts to dispel his jock image.

Roy was a broken-toothed Cockney, from the docks of London's tough East End. He had long, dirty blond hair cut in a raggedy page boy haircut. He had been the original bass player with the seminal rock band Savoy Brown. As the band had become more sophisticated they had let him go.

Gurdjieff Dave was a mystery man of working class origins. He was in his early thirties, and had lived a life on the road for many years. He was self-educated, and supposedly highly intelligent. None of us saw much of him at first, as he spent his days sleeping in a dirty nest of blankets and his nights reading until dawn in esoteric texts on magic, psychology, and philosophy. He turned out to be a bit of a power tripper, sort of a nonviolent Charles Manson, and the commune split into those who considered him an inspired genius and leader, and those who thought him a dirty, unkempt nuisance.

People kept drifting in from all over the world. Two brothers, Odd Job and Little Brother, came all the way from Australia. Odd Job was built like a fire hydrant, and had supposedly been a biker in the Australian Hell's Angels. Little Brother was his younger brother, a mischievous sixteen-year-old who at least managed to keep a small motorbike running, unlike his transportless brother. Odd Job's girlfriend also moved in. Mouse was a typical biker chick, and as nondescript as her name.

Colin also arrived from Australia. He had a young daughter, Melissa, about five years old. Colin looked like an aging surfer, and he gave off an air of perpetual amazement at the goings-on in the hotel. Some people would always retain an air of "straightness" about them, and Colin was a good example.

Christos arrived one evening, all curly freaked-out hair and handsome dark Spanish looks. He had left Spain to avoid their military draft, and it was humourous to hear his attempts at English which became even more fractured with his increased dope smoking. He soon took up with a gorgeous dark English girl, and eventually they got married.

There were only a limited number of rooms, and soon people began sharing the tiny quarters. Many were traditional male-female couples, but others were very odd matches. Billy was an easy-going waiter from L'Auberge. His roommate was Scotch John, a tough former construction foreman from the roughest part of Glasgow. Most of us waited for Scotch John to pummel Billy, as we often heard him swearing at him in his tough brogue, but somehow peace and goodwill prevailed, and they shared a room for years.

Through thin walls
radio blaring
"It's All Right Now"

Chapter 9
Alice

I settled in my little room, which had done duty as a storage closet in the hotel's earlier incarnations. It was the first room on the right at the top of the stairs on the top floor. The dimensions were roughly six feet wide by about twelve feet long. There was a little window overlooking the derelict front yard of the hotel.

The hotel had three floors. The ground floor was divided into several huge rooms, which had been bars and dining areas. The second floor was a warren of rooms, and it had the only bathtub in the hotel, as well as a small kitchen.

One night I was poking about downstairs in the kitchen and I met this somewhat odd looking young woman of about my age with big tits. I was getting a lot of female attention, now that my hair was growing thick and long and freaky and I was a founding member of the Eel Pie Island commune. With my brave new ego, I tried chatting up this visitor, whose name was Alice. For some macho reason I jokingly lifted her, and carried her upstairs to my little room. When I got her upstairs, I immediately let her go, but she said, "So, aren't you going to finish what you started?" "I was only kidding around," I hedged. But she wanted more. We started necking, and soon we were naked. She had lovely big breasts and sleek black hair. She looked like she had Indian blood, like some sort of Aztec fertility doll come to life. She was a lot hornier and more experienced than Jools, and she was very wet when I entered her. After a minute or two I was ready to come, and she told me to pull out. And so I learned the rhythm method.

When I pulled out milliseconds before my orgasm, she continued humping my cock with her full belly, and I shot my hot sperm all over her round stomach:

**Pulling out
coming against
her rising belly**

Later that night she wanted sex again and I was happy to oblige. This time she told me to hold back, that she wanted it to last longer. Somehow I was able to hold back, and I kept pumping away until she said that the walls were moving for her. She moaned, "Now you're learning how to satisfy a woman. That was better!"

**Old mattress
smelling of mould, cum
and incense**

Chapter 10
Eel Pie Days

Life as a draft resisting hippie was becoming more tolerable. Most evenings we stayed up until the wee hours smoking incredibly strong three-paper joints of tobacco and hash and sucking on hash-stuffed chillums. Sometimes there were impromptu musical jams. Many could play, or attempted to play, guitar. We would all sing, until finally we lapsed into stoned reveries.

Those who had a lot of sexual frustration to work out organized a sex room. Despite my interest, I only visited the orgy room once in its heyday, and only as a voyeur. The unventilated room was so thick with the smell of spunk and sweat that it put me off, and I didn't have the confidence to perform in front of everybody.

And so the evenings and nights were spent in stoned bliss. I wouldn't get up until mid to late afternoon, and then I'd wander across the bridge to the Linton Cafe. It was a narrow workers' cafe which served healthy portions of bacon and eggs and toast and tea for only three shillings and sixpence. There was a small dining room upstairs, overlooking the alley leading up from the embankment and the bridge, and often the room was filled with Eel Piers eating their one meal of the day:

Bacon and eggs
in a workers' cafe
at teatime

After noshing at the Lynton, I would often walk back along the Thames embankment and watch the ducks swimming. The path led past the ancient Anglican churchyard and up several stairs carved in stone to an elevated promenade.

A gate in the hedges opened into a botanical gardens for a stately house, which was public property. There were three rectangular garden areas, bordered by high trees. A magnificent artificial waterfall splashed into a pond overseen by a statue of Venus surrounded by naked nymphs. Often I would sit in the lotus position beside a small fish pond and meditate on the beautiful scene.

Other days I would wander into the greenhouse, which had flowers blooming all year round. Sometimes I would follow the towpath a couple of miles into Richmond. It was a pleasant walk, and it led past old boats moored under weeping willows. Most days I found the walk idyllic, but occasionally I had a down day, and amplified by all the hashish even the ducks and swans and weeping willows wouldn't lift my spirits during the walk.

stoned and depressed
dogshit on the towpath

Those days were rare, however. When I got to Richmond I would cross Richmond Bridge, and sometimes stop at L'Auberge for tea. I wasn't as interested in L'Auberge now that I had the scene in the hotel, and often I would continue up Richmond Hill with its vistas and gardens and stroll into Richmond Park.

Sometimes I would take the back streets of Richmond, and enter the park by the back gate. Once into the park I felt free again, and would walk for hours. The park stretched for miles, and there weren't many other people on weekdays. Sometimes I would find a secluded spot and meditate, or take out my notebook and write poetry.

Yellow
butterflies, flowers
leaves

Vine
leaves pressing
church window

washing up
in a public washroom
hobo likes my singing

Chapter 11
The Buddhist Monastery

Mark Valiant at first seemed an unlikely person to have a deeply religious side. He was an ex-cop, and the story goes that as he was becoming more and more sympathetic towards the youth rebellion, one day he took the plunge, and took it in a big way. Mark took a strong dose of STP, a psychedelic even more hallucinatory than LSD. He tripped for three days, and after that experience he was a changed man. He quit the police, grew a beard and took to hanging around L'Auberge Cafe.

Mark was one of the regulars in Martha's crowd, sort of an older brother for Martha and a surrogate son for the Holmes. He had been the unofficial "elder" who took charge when Martha's parents left on their holiday to Ibiza, the one I ruined with the flooding bathtub.

A couple of times Mark led Sunday expeditions to a Buddhist monastery several miles away. It was always exciting to get up early for a change, and to watch London slowly coming to life from the top deck of a double-decker bus.

A path led down a lane to the monastery and the temple beside it. The service consisted of all present sitting in meditation in the comfortable chapel for about a half hour or forty-five minutes. It was very relaxing, and the meditations were led by a monk, who sat in front. The layout of the chapel and pews wasn't that dissimilar from a Christian service - with the notable difference that no words were spoken, no hymns sung. It was up to each of us to make our peace with the world.

One morning a cat found its way into the chapel, and halfway through meditation it let out a yowl, and decided it wanted to go elsewhere. It was amusing to see the startled look on all our faces at this unexpected interruption, but the monk calmly got up and let the cat out to wander off, and we resumed meditating.

My impression of these mornings is of a tranquil blue atmosphere. There was a subtle presence of blue energy always present after we had begun meditating, and my feeling was that the monk was pleased with the aura, which I'm sure he was very aware of.

After the meditation session we would gather in the vestibule of the chapel, and drink tea and discuss religion. Everyone present was offered an equal chance to speak, either to pose or to answer questions offered by the others present. Not surprisingly, after the relaxing effects of the meditation, most of us didn't have much to say, the words would have just come between us and the immediacy of the experience of sitting calmly in the blue atmosphere of the chapel.

One Sunday morning in early winter, when I was making one of my last visits to the chapel with a couple of other Eel Piers, it began to snow. Many years later I still clearly remember the experience of walking down the narrow lane, crunching the white powder under my scuffed boots, when this haiku popped into my mind:

**Walking to meditation
through fresh snow**

Chapter 12
The Schoolgirls

The derelict Eel Pie ballroom was opened for business once again. It looked like a high school gym done over by hippies. There were garish psychedelic paintings all over the flaking walls. The most striking was the looming head of a red-eyed hippie king, with his Aubrey Beardsley tresses winding about the walls. He made Charles Manson look almost benevolent by comparison, and the longer I lived in the hotel, the more I felt I looked like him. My quick-growing black hair was getting longer and freakier and my scraggly beard was beginning to fill in.

Friday and Saturday night were band nights. A young, hip and bi-sexual entrepreneur was booking rock bands from all over Great Britain. Some of the groups went on to fame as name acts, such as Atomic Rooster. The Edgar Broughton Band, the band which had preceded my visit to the 144 Piccadilly squat, also paid a visit. Legend had it that the Eel Pie ballroom was one of The Rolling Stones' early venues, and the ballroom was continuing to play an important role in the developing careers of many breaking bands.

These wild weekend affairs, the great mouldy room with the paint splattered walls and the bottles of beer being sold from battered fridges, attracted all manner of hippies and trendies and students and – oh joy was me – schoolgirls!

While the band thrashed away, a light show floated over the crazily dancing crowd and the band from a projection booth high at the other end of the hall. Many of the people were high on hash and speakeasy beer, and more than a few on acid and speed and Mandrax, the "mandies make you randy" quaalude of the London drug scene. To this inspired debauchery ventured the braver of the Richmond and Twickenham schoolgirls. They would come in packs, and many of them were gorgeous young English roses of fifteen or sixteen.

I already knew a few students from L'Auberge, and apparently many of the girls already knew of me. I was becoming "Canadian Chris", an Eel Pie denizen with black Irish good looks and a romantic past as a 'Miami Beach hippie' and a cohort of swash-buckling Canadian Peter. For the first time in my life I was in demand by women, beautiful young women who were in the process of their own sexual revolutions!.

I flopped with the first one I lured back to my room. She was one of the most gorgeous young women I had ever seen; with her blonde hair and pouting lips she looked like a young Brigitte Bardot. She was with a crowd of her girlfriends, and I quickly singled her out. She was as pleased to be selected by the notorious Canadian Chris as I was to win the attention of the most attractive girl in the hall. When I got her back to my cubbyhole, we wasted no time in stripping. She had the most perfect body I had ever seen - she had that soft always-tanned skin some blonde women have, and the firmest, most perfectly cupped breasts with pouty aureoles. We rubbed our bodies in the dark, but I just couldn't get hard enough, or brave enough to enter this fantasy woman. I even dated her a few times after this, but her parents quickly whisked her away on a vacation to Scotland.

The next schoolgirl was Lesley. She wasn't nearly as gorgeous as the first one, but she was slim and brown haired and intelligent. She was also a virgin, and dying to lose her virginity. Europeans have probably always had a more tolerant attitude towards sex, and this nubile teenager was anxious to start getting her share. For some reason she had a boyfriend who was reluctant to take her virginity, and so she had come to Eel Pie to find a man of the world such as me to solve her problem.

To woo her I recited as much of *The Eve of St. Agnes* as best I could remember, and then I hammed up the rest of a mediaeval seduction scene, where I was a shepherd and she was the desirable young princess or some such. It was a great fantasy, and I had no problem entering her stretched young body as a climax to our play.

The next day she returned to the commune with some cans of food for me, to look after her hippie/gypsy/poet lover.

Friday night
schoolgirls follow music
over Eel Pie bridge

Chapter 13

Dominic and the Gnome Homes

One of the most interesting characters in Eel Pie, both in looks and personality, was Dominic. He had a flaming orange Afro, a bulbous nose and crinkly blue eyes. Dominic liked to wear gherkins and other medieval outfits, and he truly looked like a modern-day, full-sized gnome.

He was from Liverpool, where he bragged of being a regular at the Cavern, the club made famous for being the launching pad for The Beatles.

One Sunday afternoon, as a girlfriend and I were coming out of my room, we ran into Dominic. In his thick, Scouse accent he was burbling, "You won't believe what I've just found. Little gnome houses, a whole path of gnome houses on a winding lane. They'll trip you out! Go through the little gate just before the bridge and you'll see them."

We weren't sure if Dominic was on an acid trip, but his description was so fascinating we decided to take a look. We were dubious about opening the rickety wire gate with the posted sign "RESIDENTS ONLY", but we were too intrigued to be put off. Sure enough, there they were, just as Dominic had described them with his painter's eye. The dainty path led past hobbit house after house. Little bungalows not much bigger than dog houses. Some of the bungalows were painted bright colours, many had elaborate gingerbread wood decorations, and all were immaculately landscaped.

Some of them looked hardly big enough for a human to enter. There were about ten or fifteen houses on each side of the path. The last house was slightly bigger than the others, and it had a large dovecote in the side yard.

Later I learned that most of the cottages were inhabited by retired seniors, which added to the otherworldly charm of hobbit row. In 1985 my brother and I returned to England to bury our father's ashes, and we paid a visit to Eel Pie. The site of the hotel had been turned into a condominium development, ironically named "Aquarius". On the way back off the island, I checked by the little gate. Sure enough hobbit row was still there, and we were relieved that the spirit of Eel Pie was still being represented by something other than a trendy condo development:

Dove white
against Thames brown
dovecote

Chapter 14
Twickenham Cemetery

I got a letter in the early winter of 1970 from my parents informing me that 'for my own best interests' they were no longer going to send me any money. I held out for as long as I could, and then when starvation became a real likelihood, I began working for temporary manpower agencies. A day or two's work would supply enough money to last me for several weeks, and then I'd head out in the early morning dark for another menial job, usually with another Eel Pier also on the verge of starvation.

The winter and the spring passed in this manner. My temporary assignments included work in a book depository, cleaning a filthy flooded basement in a downtown office building, organizing office files and a stint sweeping floors in a textile factory.

It was a hand-to-mouth existence, but it didn't bother me too much, because at least I was alive and not dropping napalm on civilians in Vietnam. One of the L'Aubergers commented to me one day that I should get a job, as I seemed to be becoming more and more spaced out by the hippie lifestyle. Roy had been talking about applying at the Twickenham Cenetery, and so I decided to accompany him. Somehow I managed to get up early for the visit to the cemetery, but Roy didn't. I decided to go ahead with my plans, as I'd already ruined a good morning's sleep, and I might as well go for a walk on this beautiful June morning.

The Twickenham Cemetery was several miles away, and I enjoyed the early summer walk. To my great surprise, I was hired on the spot, and a pair of garden shears were handed to me and I was told to clip the grass around the graves in the plot by the entrance. I realized that this was a test, and I bent my back and went to work. It was peaceful in the cemetery, and very relaxing stooping among the trees and gravestones, many of which were a hundred years old or more.

The morning passed pleasantly, although I was beginning to feel faint, as I didn't have any money for food, and I hadn't eaten. I hummed Rolling Stones' songs to keep my mind off hunger, and by the end of the day I'd clipped my way through half the plot. Just as I was finishing, two of the local schoolgirls appeared - Lesley, of *Eve of St Agnes* memories, and her pretty girlfriend, Carol. They had gone to visit me at the Hotel, where someone had told them that I had gone to the cemetery to find work. The two nubile girls must have made quite an impression on the other workmen, and I sailed off at five o'clock weak with hunger but accompanied by my two sexy friends.

And so began my induction into the working class. To be at work by 8 am required that I get up by seven, and that meant getting to bed before midnight. No more all night dope sessions. I bought a second-hand bicycle, and the three mile ride each morning was just about enough to wake me up before I reached the cemetery.

The days fell into a pleasant routine. A couple of hours clipping the dewy grass, and then into our shed for ten o'clock tea. A quick flip through the daily tabloids, and then back to the grass and birds and flowers until lunch. For lunch I'd bike into the nearby hamlet and have bacon and eggs at a workers' cafe. Some days I'd bring a bag of nuts and raisins and a juice, and spend a relaxing hour lounging in the sun in the park-like setting of the cemetery:

Breaktime
coal smoke, thermos tea
tabloid ink

The fifty or so acres of the cemetery were surrounded by a low fence completely overgrown by a privet hedge. There were five of us working full time, so the grounds were immaculately gardened.

George was the foreman. He took his job seriously, but he was an open-minded and tolerant boss, and so long as we did our jobs, he didn't interfere.

Fred was a rough-looking character - he had a ferocious look about him, like a living caricature of an axe murderer. His thick black brows almost covered his sunken eyes, and his body was ill-shaped but extremely strong looking. Fred was a gravedigger, and he looked as if he didn't wash off the dirt from his labours for weeks at a time. I soon learned that under his coarse exterior beat the proverbial heart of gold, and Fred wouldn't hurt a fly.

His mate was Tom, a sly character with whom I never established any rapport. Lanny was our other mate. He was simple minded and lazy, and the story was that he had never been the same since his father had been blasted to bits right in front of him during the blitz in World War Two. Lanny was amiable enough if you left him alone, and very quiet.

As the days fell into a comfortable pattern, so the year itself took on its seasonal changes. After a few months I was promoted from full time headstone clipper to part time grass mower. As a teenager I had earned pocket money mowing neighbours' lawns, and I had always enjoyed a Zen sense of fulfillment in the work.

The long London fall was spent raking and burning piles of leaves. We'd load up the hand-pulled cart, surely a relic from another century, and then the lucky assigned person would pitch the leaves and wreaths and dead flowers onto the bonfire. It was pleasant to work in front of the roaring fire and keep warm while enjoying the aromatic smoke:

Fall bonfire
crackling leaves
and dead flowers

In winter we had fewer chores. The grass stopped growing, the leaves were all raked, and our main chore was the planting of trees for the spring:

In the dead of winter
planting trees
in the graveyard

Spring comes early in London. By late January the first bulbs, snowdrops, are pushing through. Quickly they are followed by the many coloured crocuses. By mid-March the daffodils and tulips are up, and spring is in full bloom.

A grammar school was across the road from the cemetery. One of my spring highlights was the day two of the young mini-skirted beauties wandered over on their lunch break to look for rabbits. One girl was a gorgeous brunette, and her girlfriend was a blonde. They were all of fourteen years old, and they were as interested in meeting the cemetery "hairy" as I was in flirting with these beautiful distractions. It became a custom for the three of us to meet on our lunches and talk.

Spring was also the signal for the neighbourhood gardeners to begin work. The area was a poor, working-class district. Most of the local houses were council row houses without gardens, but a plot had been set aside behind the cemetery for allotment gardens:

Behind the graveyard
senior citizens digging
allotment gardens

Summer brought a couple of summer student workers. They were looked upon as a necessary nuisance by the older workers, and so George assigned me to be their "ganger". We had a great time. Tony was Anglo-Indian, and an accomplished folk singer who had performed gigs at the Hanging Lantern Cafe in Richmond. We would trade lines from Bob Dylan songs while we worked, and the days went by more quickly than ever:

Summer students
shouting Dylan
across graves

Working in the cemetery was almost vacation enough, although I did take a month off that spring and fly to the Balearic Islands off the coast of Spain. These adventures are told later.

Eel Pie was also entering its final days. The junkyard landlord had repeatedly tried to get us out, but to no avail. However, natural processes were destroying the "commune" both physically and spiritually. Floor boards had been ripped up for two winters, and the very foundations of the hotel had been weakened. Lead had been stripped off the roof and sold to metal dealers. While Eel Piers were slowly demolishing the building bit by bit, more and more wandering hippies, musicians, runaways and finally junkies and bikers moved in.

Most of the original Eel Piers moved on to more secure squats in the heart of London, but I stayed on. The bikers took to throwing stones through all the windows, and syringes could now be found littering the dirt-packed floors.

Finally I packed it in too, and my final months at the cemetery were spent boarding in a crowded rooming house for Irish navvies. I had spent the full cycle of a year working in Twickenham Cemetery. It was time to take to the road, to find the romance and excitement that had sustained me in other places, with other people:

Green garden hose
spouting
a rainbow

Dewdrop
in spiderweb
on graveyard gate

Chapter 15
The Clap Clinic

Almost all the hippies in Eel Pie were very sexually active. Sean even drew up a list of males who 'should be castrated' and posted it. I was near the top.

Fuckbucket Flo put the rest of us to shame. She was an older waitress, more of a slattern than a hippie, who discovereed she could have all the sex she wanted in the Eel Pie Hotel.

One night she ended up in my room. She wasn't attractive, with dishwater hair and a rangy figure, but I was horny and she was available. After we were both naked I could smell a bad odour in her sex. Our mutual performances were uninspired, just two horny people.

Gypsy Linda was living in my room, and a few nights later I tried to have sex with her. For an Eel Pie resident she wasn't sexually promiscuous, but as she was attracted to me, she let me rub my cock up and down her thighs and ejaculate on her full bum. During the rubbing my cock felt itchy, and this added to the sensation. But when I came, there was a brief, agonizing pain. I thought his was just from getting off in a more frictional method than usual, and fell asleep.

I awoke early the next morning and made my way downstairs to relieve myself. I attempted to urinate, and almost passed out. The searing pain was so strong, I couldn't let the urine go, although my bladder was screaming for release. I remembered the cliché of pain so great it felt like 'pissing razor blades', and I realized that I had a dose of the clap, gonorrhea.

In a sleepy haze I got dressed, and then found another awake Eel Pier to ask directions to the out patient clap clinic. The pain was so overriding there was no question of delaying.

After sitting in agony in the waiting room of the public clinic, I was soon ushered into the doctor's office. He was a nervous man with fastiduous manners, and as he pulled on his rubber gloves, he told me to lower my trousers.

With a weird little smile on his face, he took hold of my cock. His mannerisms and suppressed giggle made me think he must be a closet homosexual, who enjoyed this legitimate chance to come in contact with young male genitals. I didn't care what sort of perverse enjoyment he was getting from closely inspecting my cock, I just had to be cured.

He took a swab and inserted it in the opening of my cock. Again I just about passed out. After a few questions, he quickly diagnosed gonorrhea, and gave me a shot of penicillin. I remember the relief being almost immediate. When I attempted to urinate, it was an incredible relief to be able to pass water again.

The lab analysis also showed I was infected with non-specific urethritis, NSU, an infection as vague as its name. The penicillin had cleared up the gonorrhea, but I had to take tablets for the NSU for several weeks, and of course refrain from sex.

I had suffered agonies of pain, but even worse I had also unknowingly infected several young girls.

Used condoms
crumble on a ledge
fall leaves

Chapter 16
Tripping

Many of the communards were heavily into LSD trips. I was wary of the group trips, both because I didn't trust the motives of some involved, and also because the effects of too much acid were becoming apparent to me.

A sad case was Mark. He and his girlfriend Andrea spent most of the time locked in their room. Mark was tall and thin, with a narrow, very pale face. He looked like a mime, doing an impression of a hippie. He had always been theatrical, and the acid must have stripped away the already thin boundaries that separated fantasy from reality. The stories of his irrational antics grew. In a self-styled guerilla theatre gesture he had stolen dresses from a ladies shop in the very working class Twickenham. He was always yelling off-key rock'n'roll lyrics, and wandering around the hotel in a daze.

One night Mark stumbled into my room in the middle of the night. I was asleep, and I awoke to find Mark naked and hovering above me. He was whispering something. "Egg, Egg" he was repeating. In his hands he cradled a hard-boiled egg. The mysteries of life were being revealed to him on acid, and he wanted to share the discovery with me:

Awakening
to a naked man
with a peeled egg

Another story was that Mark had befriended Peter Townshend, leader of the famous rock group The Who. Part of the story was true, because a 16-track recorder appeared in one of the rooms at Eel Pie, loaned by Townshend. Listening to it one day, I could make out the faint sounds of the Who's rock opera *Tommy* still ghosted on the tape. Townshend's house was on the embankment at the foot of the Eel Pie bridge. The story went that Mark had taken to visiting Townshend on his nocturnal wanderings, and Townshend initially found Mark interesting, possible as some sort of acid savant. Their friendship didn't last long, though, the story going that Mark had made a pass at Townshend's wife, and the volatile Townshend had chased Mark back across the bridge with an axe!

Other events made me wary of acid. Indian Alex was a self-styled nature freak. He lived on a vegetarian diet, scrounging castoff produce from the bins behind the Twickenham grocery stores. He would add nuts and berries which he found in the woods and mix up salad and rice dishes. One evening many of the Eel Piers were enjoying the effects of a group acid trip on the front lawn, lounging by the river to put on a show for any passing boaters, when Indian Alex began convulsing. The trippers gathered around, and in their stoned state they thought Alex was experiencing some form of religious ecstacy. "Wow, man, what a far-out trip that guy's on!"

Alex had accidentally mixed some hemlock root into his evening meal, and had gone into epileptic seizure. Fortunately a few of us weren't stoned on acid, and called an ambulance. Alex had to be hospitalized, but he survived, although his front teeth were knocked out by the medics during his seizure.

Acid had a freeing effect on most people for the first few trips, but for those with mental problems, the acid quickly worsened their state. It had a similar effect on group dynamics. The effects of a strong hallucinatory trip were so overwhelming that some people looked for leadership at any cost to free them from the confusion. A few of the Eel Piers, such as Magic Mike, were only too happy to assume the mantle of acid guru.

One night shouting awoke me. I was heavily stoned from smoking hash, and in a mood of stoned susceptibility. The noise was coming from downstairs, and I went to investigate. Magic Mike and other Eel Piers were haranguing a new dosser. Magic Mike had worked himself up into a state of acid righteousness, and he was demanding the dosser leave. Everyone was tripped out of their minds, and the lines between reality and fantasy had blurred, because Magic Mike and the others were talking cosmic nonsense, a sort of acid fascism. In my stoned state some of it even made sense to me, and when I started to intervene on behalf of the dosser, who only seemed to want a place to stay, Magic Mike started screaming, "Nature is here! I feel the presence of nature! Who is representing nature?"

I knew I was being addressed. From the communal trips those present had assumed cosmic personalities, and as everyone knew how much I loved nature and knew about my haiku poems, I knew that Magic Mike was challenging me. I had been in the commune longer than any of those present, and I still had cachet because of this, and so I let the dosser sleep in my room, away from the ravings of the self-styled acid fascists. The commune was changing for the worse, and much of the problem was the acid:

LSD
these clouds reveal too much
moon

Chapter 17

Formentera

To escape the psychedelic nonsense of Eel Pie and the routine of the graveyard, I decided to visit the Balearic Islands in the Mediterranean Sea off Spain. I caught a tourist flight to the island of Majorca, where the Holmes family took their vacations. There I hooked up with some Spanish street kids, and together we caught a ferry to the hippie island of Ibiza. After spending the night on a rocky beach, I decided to catch the ferry to the even more remote and mysterious island of Formentera:

Sleeping in ruins
La Guardia's flashlight
signals false dawn

By midday I was standing on the ferry's rolling deck eating fresh figs and watching the mountainous shape of Formentera come into focus. After disembarking I walked the couple of miles up the straight and flat only road road into the main hamlet, which consisted of the bar Fonda Pepe, a hostel, a bakery and a couple of houses.

I wasn't to meet Mette, a Scandinavian girl I had met in Majorca, until the next evening, and so I set off to explore the island. I met up with a German student on holiday, and he invited me back to his villa. The only tourists to have discovered Formentera were the Germans, apart from itinerant artists and hippies from all over the world. The student talked about psychology, and then he wanted to sunbathe nude. I got a bisexual vibe, and politely made my exit as soon as I could. I continued following the dirt track. There was only the occasional farmhouse, and soon I reached the sea.

The path became more rocky and began to climb. Finally it ended and I followed the hilly rim of the sea. There were no houses now, and I walked some miles with the hypnotic sea crashing hundreds of feet below me. It had been a day full of excitement and fresh sea air, and when I reached what seemed to be the highest and most remote part of the island, night was falling. Luckily, I found a small cave in the cliffs, and tucking my possessions under my head, I fell asleep with my feet in the cave and my head on the ledge hundreds of feet above the Mediterranean.

The sun awoke me early on my perch, and when I looked down into the clear sea, I saw a shark lazily undulating by:

Below the cliffs
shark undulating
clear morning sea

I packed my things and wandered in the direction I hoped town to be. I stopped at a well by a farmhouse, and the old farmer spoke enough English to hold a conversation. He had been a merchant seaman, and had retired to the outback of Formentera, his home island.

After several hours of walking, I found my way back to Fonda Pepe, where I joined the international throng of hippies, writers, wanderjahr students and hip Spaniards. We sat in a long, raggle-taggle line on the verandah outside the cafe, drinking beer we couldn't afford and chatting. A full-bodied blonde hitchhiker from Germany seemed quite interested in this English hippie, but the cold sores around her mouth put me off. We sat and drank with our feet on a little railing, watching the awesome sunset over the beautifully barren landscape of Formentera.

Later that evening Mette showed up, as good as her word. We went off and rented a room in the pensione, where they made us keep our passports in their safe.

The next day we roamed around looking for a house to rent. This was a dharma time for me, and I met an American who was about to return to the States. He offered to let me rent the farmhouse he had been living in, as he still had a month's rent left. I paid him a few hundred pesetas, and Mette and I prepared to move in the next day. The farmhouse was a beautiful stone building, with a well in front and the name "Maria Jerome" painted over the front door. There were only three rooms, a kitchen, a bedroom and a den with an open fireplace, but to us it was a mansion:

Wellwater
constellations
sesame seeds in honey

Maria Jerome faced one of the ubiquitous foot trails on the island. There was a sparse forest across from the house, and the cottage itself was surrounded by its own fields, and the flower-filled fields of the neighbouring farmer. The only other farmhouse was about two hundred yards away, and then a hilly vista of fields stretched all the way to the sea, about a mile and a half away. On clear days you could even see Ibiza, and the "singing rocks" that stand guard that legend has Ulysses passed on his voyage where the sirens tried to lure his ship to ruin with their unearthly singing.

There was no runnning water, and the only toilet facilities were to squat by one of the rock fences that mazed around the house. Propriety dictated that after shitting in the field, one covers one's business with a rock. A poem for the most enjoyable shits I have taken in my life:

FORMENTERA SHIT ASANA

Squatting in the ozone air
by the rock field fence
tiny perfect flowers at my feet

across the cool blue Med
the Siren Rocks of Ibiza
sing through these dancing butterflies

Mette and I moved into the cottage. Even the name seemed a good omen, Maria Jerome being the Spanish equivalents of my mother's name, Marianne, and my brother's name, Jeremy.

We slept in the bedroom the first night, all rolled up in my sleeping bag. Mette didn't seem horny, and didn't want a repeat of the drunken sex we'd had the night before in the pensione before leaving Fonda Pepe. She sneezed and hacked and sneezed, and complained that her allergies couldn't stand the dust of the farmhouse.

So Mette moved back into the pensione by herself. I was just as happy to be living in seclusion, and in a few days I acquired a couple of hippie roommates. My second or third day in Maria Jerome I wandered the mile or so into the hamlet. Coming towards me was the raunchiest, scraggliest hippie I had ever seen. He probably looked like me. He made a beeline for me, and when we said hello, it became apparent he was English. Then one of the weirdest coincidences of my life happened. Roger asked me if I had a place to put him up, and when I told him my name, his eyes opened wide and he pulled a scrap of paper from his dirty pockets. My name was written on the scrap, and the address of the Eel Pie Hotel, and rough instructions on how to find the commune.

Amazingly, Roger had met California Jon in Amsterdam, and Jon had given him my name and the Eel Pie information and told him I would put him up in London. Roger had changed his mind about going to London, and instead had made the long tour down the European coasts and then hitched across Spain, where he caught the mainland ferry for the Balearics.

While Roger was hitching south, I had decided to take the first vacation of my working career, and had taken a month's leave of absence from the Twickenham Cemetery, and also headed south. And so this incredible coincidence, Roger and I meeting on this remote island in the middle of the Mediterranean Sea! I was even able to fulfill California Jon's promise and give Roger a place to stay. The I Ching was working its mysteries.

I spent several weeks living in Maria Jerome. Some days I would walk into the little forest and chop up dead wood for our fires at night. A husband and wife pair of travelling hippies also moved in, and one night we had a party with wine and candles and a blazing fire. I remember running wild through the starry night and working off any chance of a hangover the next day.

Other days were spent reading and wandering. An old American beatnik had settled on Formentera, and to eke out an existence, he had opened a nickel-a-day library of paperback books. I discovered the works of Kurt Vonnegut, and you couldn't have chosen a better setting for reading his classics *Sirens of Titan* and *Slaughterhouse Five*, with the flights of fantasy and incredible coincidences and ironies that are Vonnegut's stock in trade. I felt I was living a life as romantic and exciting as many of his characters.

Other coincidences happened, as well as finding Marie Jerome and Roger. An American hippie I met at Fonda Pepe had dated a girl I had a crush on in high school, and I learned that she had gone on to become a fashion model. He also moved into Maria Jerome for a few days.

Every day I threw the I Ching, and one day its message was "it is propitious to cross the waters". I didn't question the meaning, as my idyll was due to come to an end. I left Maria Jerome in the care of the other hippies, and walked the long, narrow path down to the ferry.

Chapter 18

The Night The Hog Farmers
Got Swamped

One fine summer evening a whole travelling commune came to visit Eel Pie. The Hog Farmers were a famous American commune. One of their leaders, Wavy Gravy, had been the main announcer at the Woodstock Festival.

The Hog Farmers set up a huge teepee on the front lawn, overlooking the Thames. Other Hog Farmers camped in smaller tents, and the hotel took on an even more raffish and carnival-like atmosphere than usual. Most of us squeezed into the Hog Farm teepee to share hash and stories with our American brothers and sisters. The Hog Farmers were full of themselves, a trait familiar to the British who suffered an invasion of the liberating 'Yanks' during the latter part of World War II. But the mood that night was of brotherhood and camaraderie inside the huge teepee.

I went to bed very late, and slept in until mid-afternoon, as usual. When I finally made it downstairs, an odd sight met me. Thirty or so soaked Hog Farmers were spread out on the ground floor of the hotel. They were even more disheveled and bedraggled than usual.

I ran into Seamus and asked what had happened. "The tidal bore came through last night," he told me with a grin. "It only happens once or twice a year. A great big wall of water is forced up the Thames by the pressure of the tides. Our lucky Hog Farmers, so in touch with the forces of nature, picked the one night of the year to camp on our lawn when the tidal bore hit. It swept up about three feet into the yard, and washed all the Hog Farmers into the hotel in the middle of the night."

Beside the Thames
giant teepee
spilling hippies

Chapter 19
Skinheads

I first encountered skinheads at the 144 Piccadilly squat. They were the antithesis of hippies - they had shaven heads and they wore deliberately drab working class garb - usually jeans with suspenders and steel-toed Doc Marten boots. The boots were their signature - the steel toes were for doing damage to their opponents in street fights. While hippies, or "hairies" as the skinheads called us, stood for peace and love and generally left-liberal values, the skinheads represented a twisted set of working class values - they were against immigration, drugs, rock music and their perceived softness of middle class values. Some skinheads were from the tough, working class East End, while others were the lumpen, the children of welfare parents and the dregs of English society.

For some reason British teens have a tendency to divide themselves into identifiable groups. In the 1950s the rebels were the working class 'Teddy Boys', and in the early 60s there had been riots between the 'rockers', who rode motorcycles and liked rock'n'roll, and the 'mods', who rode motor scooters and wore their hair carefully styled. So the division into skinheads and hippies was part of a British tradition, a confused byproduct of a still heavily class-stratified society, where everyone is assigned a role.

There were exceptions, of course. Some hippies were from working class backgrounds, and a few skinheads were middle class poseurs. There were many ironies in the dictated fashions of the two groups -

the often racist skinheads preferred listening to reggae music, a product of black Caribbean musicians, and many hippies preferred a muddled socialism, which is the politics of the working class.

The skinheads espoused violence, fighting amongst themselves in their pubs, and sometimes practising particularly violent and racist attacks on coloured immigrants, which they called 'Paki bashing'. Of course hippies were a favourite target of the skinheads, who liked nothing better than to bash up a pacifist longhair. 'Gay bashing' along the Thames' towpaths, long an established haunt for London homosexuals, was another trademark activity of the skins.

Usually I managed to avoid confrontations with the skinheads. They mostly stuck to their pubs and parts of town, and the hippies frequented the drug-tolerant pubs and cafes and the parks and places like the Eel Pie Hotel. Occasionally there were clashes, usually when a gang of skinheads came upon a lone hippie. This only happened to me twice. Once a girlfriend and I were walking in Green Park in downtown London, when we saw a swarm of people coming towards us. It was a Sunday, and we thought it must be a large group of picnickers. It wasn't until the swarm was almost upon us that we realized it was a huge gang of hundreds of skinheads. I thought it best to ignore them and to not show any fear. The skinheads were mostly young, only around fifteen or sixteen.

When they reached us, they started shouting "Bring up the scissors, we've got a couple of hairies!" I suspected this was a bluff, and then the skins began kicking me, but not really hard at first, with their steel-toed boots. Then I saw one start to kick at my girlfriend, and I yelled "Stop kicking a chick!" There was an embarrassed pause when the skins realized how unchivalrous they were being by assaulting a woman, even a hairy, and they let us pass.

My second encounter with skins had the potential for even more danger. One of the regular visitors at the hotel was a young local girl with long, frizzy blonde hair. I offered to drive her home late one night on my bicycle, and the chain broke. On my way back from her house I was wheeling my disabled bike, with the broken chain in my hands, when a car full of skinheads pulled alongside and rolled down their windows.

These were older skins, in their late teens and early twenties, and they seemed much more violent than the young kids in Green Park. "Hey, mate, want to play some football!" the skins taunted, as they began to spill out of the car. As they started to pile out to do a gang number on me, they noticed for the first time the chain dangling in my hands. Suddenly not so brave, they piled back into their car and skidded out of sight.

Almost all the hippies in Eel Pie were non-violent, the exception being Scotch John. Scotch John had grown up in the Gorbals, the toughest part of Glasgow. Before becoming a hippie, he had been the foreman of a construction crew, and in this tough environment Scotch John had become a master of 'the Glasgow bop'. The Glasgow bop is a spin-off from soccer playing, where experienced players field the ball with headers off the strong bone structures of their foreheads.

To perform the bop, John would grab an opponent by both shoulders, and then smack the victim's nose with his forehead, usually breaking their nose and making a bloody mess of their face. Scotch John had a personality as aggro as the staunchest skinhead, and stories were told of his walking into the Twickenham skinhead pub, The Crows Nest. Most of us would scuttle past the Crows Nest on the far side of the street, and a few Eel Piers had been roughed up and dumped in the Thames by the Crows Nest regulars. So when Scotch John sauntered into the busy pub, he was followed by a trail of amused skins into the washroom. BOP! BOP BOP BOP and it was all over. After Scotch John's foray into skinhead turf, most of us were treated with more respect by the skins, as they probably couldn't tell the rest of us from Scotch John, who had the standard shoulder length black hair and beard, bellbottom jeans and a leather-fringed jacket.

In a courtyard
skinheads
plucking flowers

Chapter 20
The Three Fishes

Pub life in London reflected the British tendency to divide into classes and areas of interest. There were upper class pubs, right wing pubs, Irish Republican pubs, working class pubs, and one unique pub where all the regulars were very short, young males who only listened to Eddie Cochran on the juke box. There were skinhead pubs and of course hippie pubs.

The Three Fishes was a hippie pub, located on the corner next to the Kingston-Upon-Thames rail station. The lights were dim, the music blaring rock'n'roll, and the clientele longhairs of both sexes. At that time in Britain, kids as young as fifteen could get away with going into pubs, although the legal drinking age was eighteen, so there was the expected quota of schoolgirls and boys.

It was just the sort of atmosphere I loved after a hard day of digging graves. On one of my first visits, a gorgeous young girl of about sixteen came and knelt before me, as if before a medieval knight. She clasped her long hippie shawl about herself, and even I found I couldn't take advantage of her, and offer the expected walk home through the park:

Young girl
in an old shawl
kneeling

One summer evening I made the long ride into Kingston on my bike after work, and had a pint or two at the Three Fishes. It stays light very late in Britain in summer, and so dusk was just turning to dark when I left after 9 p.m., and began undoing my bicycle lock.

In the half light I noticed something very strange. There were several police vans parked outside, and more arriving every second. In the dark I made out the shapes of several dozen policemen, and I realized that a raid was about to take place.

I wasn't drunk, only stupid, and some sense of hippie brotherhood won out over common sense. I walked back into the Three Fishes and began yelling "It's a raid! - It's a raid!"

The office in charge followed me through the doors, and I was the first one grabbed. "You're nicked," he snarled, and passed me to another bobby. Bustled back out the door, I caught a glimpse of the pandemonium as drugs were dumped under most of the tables. I was pushed onto a bus, much like a large tour bus, which the bobbies had requisitioned for the occasion, and soon I was joined by thirty or forty other longhairs. Then the bus and several van loads of miscreants were taken down to Kingston police headquarters and booked.

I didn't get to sleep that night, as it took the police all night to process so many of us. In the early morning light I found my way back to my locked bicycle, and slowly wound my way back towards Twickenham.

Our case didn't come up for a month, and the courtroom was a mob scene. When my turn came, I pleaded "Guilty, Your Honour" to the charge of interfering with the raid by warning everyone, but I added, "I don't feel guilty, though." The courtroom burst out laughing, both at the oddity of my charge, and at my unusual plea. I was given a fine of thirty pounds, which was then my wages for about three weeks.

Hash aroma
and stale beer
under the table

Chapter 21
Tripping To Cambridge

After watching the freak-outs around me, I decided to stay clear from the group acid trips. One of the Eel Piers had found out about a conference on communes being held on the Cambridge University campus, and so one spring morning about thirty of us piled into the back of a van and headed north.

"Canadian Chris, here's your tab of acid from the group trip yesterday," and a tab of brown acid was thrust into my hand. It wasn't possible to politely refuse, as I was going to the conference as part of the Eel Pie Community, and acid had become such an integral part of Eel Pie. I felt obligated to take the trip, but not wanting to hallucinate too much, I offered to share my tab, and Tank was only too happy to swallow half.

It was pleasant enough, sprawled on blankets and sleeping bags in the back of the van. I hoped I hadn't taken enough acid to get freaked out, and at least I had another tripper to evaluate my trip by. We drove throught the rolling countryside of Hertfordshire and Cambridgeshire, stopping once to pick up a hitchhiker.

The hitchhiker was in a time warp of his own - he was an aging Teddy Boy, wearing drainpipe trousers, winklepicker boots and his hair coiffed back à la Elvis. He was amazed by the menagerie of hippies surrounding him, and he looked relieved when he jumped off in his village.

The acid came on, not strong enough to cause full-blown hallucinations, but strong enough to cause the boundaries of my vision to waver, and to cause a mild degree of confusion and just a tinge of paranoia.

We finally arrived in Cambridge in late afternoon, and unloaded on a side street. We crossed a footbridge, where the clacking ducks made me uneasy.

Crazed quacking
iridescent ducks
tripping in Cambridge

Soon we reached the dormitory where the conference was being held. We were ushered into a large meeting room without any chairs, so we all squatted on the floor, just like back at Eel Pie. No one seemed to be in charge, and the only others present were an older couple wearing black capes. I had missed a lot of the group dynamics by being a loner, and several of the Eel Pie women began moaning nonsense lyrics, which I recognised as backing sounds from psychedelic records such as Pink Floyd's *Ummagumma*.

They were joined in their wailing by all the Eel Piers, and I found the experience discomfitting. The older couple just sat and listened to the eerie sounds. I sat uncomfortably through five or ten minutes of this, realizing that the others felt very at ease in the weird atmosphere. The room was darkened, with candles flickering. Then things got really strange. The couple got out horned goat masks and put them on. Masks were being passed around to everybody, and the atmosphere took on the aura of a black mass.

It was a complete contrast to the relaxed atmosphere I had experienced in the Buddhist chapel during morning meditations. It was time for me to leave, and I bumbled from the room.

I spent the evening in the sitting room of the dormitory, trying to focus my eyes enough to read. Through the closed doors came the moans of the Eel Piers. Another Eel Pier had also left, Blonde Chris, and he said, "Too weird for me, man, what a confusing bummer." I agreed. My days as an Eel Pier were coming to an end. What had begun as an experiment in group living and sharing was ending in the lowest common denominator, a form of group depression and psychedelic conformity, culminating in this grotesque moaning ritual.

Roomful of masks
ritual moaning
Eel Pie commune

Chapter 22
Lavenham

My father, Eric, came over to visit me one summer. He wanted to see how his son was doing, of course, and he wanted to show me Newmarket, the little town he was raised in. He had rented a car, and after visiting me in the hotel for a day or so, we drove into Suffolk, a county to the north east of London.

Like much of England, it was like driving back in time. Little villages on narrow, hedge-lined roads winding through neat fields. On the outskirts of one village we even had to drive the little Escort across a cattle crossing - the road dipped into a stream bed, and we had to slowly cross through half a foot of lazily moving trout stream:

England
sheep grazing
among gravestones

We toured Newmarket, my father's boyhood town, a picturesque village which had long been the headquarters of Britain's horse racing and breeding. For a treat he decided to show me the ancestral home of the Faiers, an even more quaint and tiny village called Lavenham. There was one main street, where the many coloured thatched houses leaned drunkenly into each other down the hill. We booked into the Swan hotel, a famous landmark often used in BBC films and tourist promotions. After dinner we strolled to one of the several local pubs. The tiny pub only seated about twenty or thirty, and on this quiet summer evening only eight or ten of the local men were slowly sipping their pints:

Lavenham
houses staggering
down main street

Eric told me that most of the people in Lavenham were named Faiers, and that afternoon we had met one or two locals who duly turned out to be distant blood relatives. The facial features were quite amazing to me, many of the people having the same narrow configuration around the nose and eyes as my father and my brother and myself.

To make his point further, my Dad asked if anyone in the pub was named Faiers. All the locals nodded assent, and then he asked, "How many of you spell Faiers F-A-I-E-R-S?" Again all nodded assent, and Eric said, "A round for all the Faierses in the house!" The locals didn't seem to mind this bit of show-boating by the dapper little Yank with his longhaired son, and everyone drank a toast to the name Faiers:

Balding father
hippie son
in an ancient pub

The next morning Eric dragged me out of bed early, and we had bacon and eggs in a cafe on the main street. We were quiet, as I was still coming to life, and as we were preparing to leave, an old gentleman who had been sipping his tea came up to us and said, "Good morning, Mr. Faiers, and Good morning to you, too, Master Faiers." One of the regulars from the pub from the night before had recognized us, and it was a welcome way to greet the morning, feeling a part of the history of a town where our family name had been the mainstay since at least 1066, when the Domesday census was collected.

Chapter 23
Hare Krishna

Martha had a redhaired friend named Jill. I always had a thing for her, and as I was in-between girlfriends, I decided to look her up. Through the grapevine I learned that she had joined the Hare Krishnas, and so one afternoon I headed downtown to their main temple with a young hippie guy who was passing through Eel Pie.

The Krishnas greeted us warmly, if a little absentmindedly. They were blissed out, in a robotic way. While we snacked on the light vegetarian food they offered us, one disciple kept repeating, "George Harrison is a member. He helps us." Over and over he name-dropped the Beatles, like a mantra.

The Krishnas ushered us into a second room, where the devotees were kneeling on mats. An incredibly ugly old man with a shaved head approached me. "I know you. We've worked together in other lives," he intoned. He seemed sincere, but I felt a little displaced. On the wall was a chart listing all the qualities of a good devotee of Krishna. Near the bottom was the word "poetic". I had always understood poetic to mean being free, to being one's own person, but the Krishnas were very dogmatic. They were better, perhaps, than the acid fascists who were taking over Eel Pie, but not by much.

Soon it was time for prayer and dancing in the chapel, a larger adjacent room. The young hippie and I followed into the chapel, and the devotees began chanting and dancing in rhythm. We joined in, not wishing to be poor guests. The effect became hypnotic, and the blue presence was in the atmosphere, just as it had been in the Buddhist Temple:

Two longhairs
among saffron & shaved heads
dancing blue phantoms

We chanted and danced for several hours, and then returned to the smaller sitting room. This alternated all afternoon. It put the two of us on a high. When we finally left in the early evening, after four or five hours of chanting, dancing and discussion, we felt very high. The blue presence was still with us, and we both wondered if the Krishnas had put small doses of acid in our vegetarian food. Although I had gone there for reasons of the flesh, I had enjoyed the afternoon, although it was too regimented for my spirit.

Years later when I received a Krishna pamphlet in Toronto, I was startled to recognize the ugly old guy with the shaved head and the cosmic memory. He was the founder of the movement, and I had been highly honoured to have had him approach me.

Chapter 24
Glastonbury Magic Festival

Word went out through the hippie grapevine of a magic festival to be held in Glastonbury. Glastonbury was a legendary sacred site in England, with a cathedral where one of the apostles had planted a rose bush which bloomed all the year round. Nearby loomed a mysterious conical hilltop, called a tor, which was rumoured to be hollow. Glastonbury Tor was said to be a 'sending station' on the system of ley lines, a power grid which lay over the English countryside, and which is the planet's equivalent of the magnetic fields which surround the human body which acupuncturists use.

Jeremy and I had earlier visited another of these mysterious tors, Michael's Mount off the Cornish Coast. Another such tor is Mont San Michel off the French coast. In the olden days festivals were held to replenish the 'dragon power', or earth magic which kept fields fertile and the inhabitants prosperous. Supposedly the twelve signs of the zodiac were laid out around Glastonbury Tor, and from the small chapel on top of the Tor one could see the zodiac's unusual shapes blended in with the English countryside.

This was an event not to be missed. The festival was to be held for the summer solstice, June 21, and I left my dossing friends in Cornwall and began to hitchhike. I got a ride as far as Salisbury, travelling quickly through the ancient fields of Stonehenge country. Walking through Salisbury, a hippie/student came up to me, and gave me a hit of acid wrapped in foil. He bragged how he and his mates had put hits of acid into the milk bottles which the local police used for their tea, and how that day a couple of cops had gone to hospital with hallucinations, while the other policemen wandered about in a happy daze all day, smiling at everyone.

I thanked him for the acid, and not knowing what to do with it, and not wanting to be caught with it in my possession after hearing his story, I put the foil packet in my mouth and resumed hitching. Rides followed quickly. First a van full of black musicians on their way to a gig picked me up, hoping to score some dope. Then a mysterious business-type man in a sleek Jaguar told me to hop in.

As we sped through the darkening evening his conversation became more and more questioning. He seemed to know a lot about the forthcoming festival, and was eager to know as much as I could tell him about it. I realized that I was beginning to babble, and then it occurred to me that the acid had been dissolving in my mouth, depite the tinfoil. So I was starting to trip, and at this point, speeding through the night, my mysterious driver told me he was the police chief for the area, and that he wanted to know what to expect from the festival goers. I tried to put his mind at ease, that we weren't going to be smuggling dope or sacrificing virgins. I also realized that I wanted to get out of the car before a full-blown acid trip took over.

He let me out on the outskirts of Piltdown, after pointing me in the general direction of the farm where the festival would be held. I wandered down the lonely highway in the dark with only starlight to guide me. The white lines in the middle of the road began stretching and blurring in an effect I knew was the result of a mild acid trip, but the effects weren't overpowering. At the juncture with the road I was to follow the next day, I slipped into a field and fell asleep, exhaustion overcoming the weak acid dose.

I awoke late the next morning, still feeling some effects from the acid, and lay in the field watching the clouds make incredible patterns in the clear blue sky.

Finally excitement at the thought of the festival overcame my lethargy, and I started to walk down the country road. Surprisingly I got another ride, this time from a local who also had heard a lot about the festival. He was dubious about the quality of our hippie magic, as the weather had been overcast for the past few days. His tone wasn't ironic, and I realized how many of the British, especially in the countryside, still believe in magic and a lot of the Celtic mythologies.

The road was becoming jammed with fellow festival goers, and when my ride let me out, I joined the throng. This was a more serious and committed type of hippie. We were the true believers for the most part, not just students growing their hair long for a wild summer.

A local farmer let us use his fields, with his stone farmhouse as headquarters. By the time I got to the site it was dinner time, and some self-styled diggers had set up a kitchen beside the farmhouse in the barnyard. I ate some stew dippped from a huge iron pot, and soon was reviving old friendships with people from the Richmond scene and elsewhere.

There was a magical excitement in the air, and the view over the festival site was typical of Somerset's hilly beauty. I wandered from the throng at the soup kitchen, and fell asleep on a hill in the middle of a field. A very odd snuffling noise awoke me very early the next morning:

Asleep in a field
a browsing cow
my alarm clock

I was too excited, for once, to fall back asleep, and made my way down the hill to where some vans were unloading around the base of an unusual structure. The rock'n'roll bands were going to play on a platform part way up a scale model of the Great Pyramid of Egypt, which we were going to build with construction scaffolding which an enlightened builder had loaned us.

Everyone was smoking dope and unloading trucks in a flurry of manic activity, and I joined in. I was proud of the muscles I had developed as a gravedigger, and I spent hours unloading scaffolding. After unloading, I joined the construction crews, and very quickly the pyramid began taking shape. For one job I had to perch on a rail high in the air and saw off the end of a piece of pipe with a hacksaw. Halfway through the job, someone handed me a carrot carved into a chillum and stuffed with pungent hash. We were a crazy looking construction crew, but somehow through the haze of hash smoke, the pyramid grew skyward. Boards were laid for the performance area, about twenty feet off the ground, and the scaffolding continued to a peak about seventy feet above that.

After working on the pyramid all day, I took off for a tour of the festival site. The farm was about a hundred acres, with hedgerows dividing the area into several major fields. Tents were appearing everywhere, and many hippies were building huts in the hedgerows. Banners and tents and colourful people were everywhere, like some medieval camp before battle.

For a bunch of spaced-out freaks, things were amazingly well organized. Six-foot deep latrines were dug, and metal pipes were laid across them. Another free kitchen sprung up towards the bottom of the site, and everyone looked like they were going to be housed and fed. At the bottom of the hilly fields, the pyramid stretched into the sky, and after several days of building, the musical part of the festival was about to begin.

I settled in a giant wigwam tent, at the bottom of the fields about a hundred yards from the pyramid. Quickly our tent became a family, and I met a blonde girl who hitched into Piltdown with me to buy food for our tribe. That night about ten of us dropped acid together while we sat huddled in blankets before the stage.

Arthur Brown was the first performer, and he tried to bum people out. He sang about how the Aquarian dream was a fake, and that we should all examine our consciences. We countered his rock star negativity by staying in our group, and whenever one of us looked a little uncomfortable, the rest of us would put our arms over them and tell them they were in a big egg and about to be reborn.

The positive group dynamics soon had us all on great acid trips, and we felt free to wander as a group. We danced and listened to the music under the stars with hundreds of other stoned worshippers, and all was at peace. Someone had gotten hold of a jug of scrumpy, a strong local cider, and that also helped ease any acid paranoias.

Later in the evening, one of us had to take a dump, and so the whole gang of us dutifully trooped over to the open air latrines, and all of us sat in a long row on the poles and had a good shit or pee, men and women, young and old. It was one of the most liberating experiences of my life, all of us sitting there in the open air under the stars, making the natural and rude noises we all must make every day of our lives without any embarrassment. Some of us got the giggles from the acid, and the relaxing sound of laughter mixed well with the rock music and the sounds of nature.

We all stumbled into the wigwam and fell asleep in each others' arms. I slept with the blonde girl, but we wanted to remain celibate to keep the spiritual atmosphere. In the middle of the night there was a commotion outside, and when we went to investigate, we noticed a giant shining star. On acid it hung in the sky like a space ship - it was the morning star, and we all stood in awe for several minutes.

After a week of wandering in the fields, listening to music around campfires and eating with our fingers, we were incredibly dirty. I decided to walk the mile to a little pond where there were thirty or forty skinnydippers splashing around. I slipped off my dirty bellbottoms, and swam around in naked bliss, the water cool under the high afternoon sun.

Late the next morning a hippie gave me a hit of acid, and then suggested we walk across the fields to Glastonbury Tor. It was a long hike, and after the usual hour the acid started coming on. It wasn't enough to overwhelm us, though. After several miles we came to a country road with a pub, and we stood and watched the swaying patterns the wind was making by sweeping through the ivy on the walls:

Wind
through ivy mat
pub walls

Finally we reached the Tor, and began the slow hike up. After twenty minutes we completed the steep climb, and there below us was laid out the Somerset countryside. Try as I might, I couldn't make out the mythical zodiac patterns, but the old chapel on the top of the Tor had a very magical aura about it, and the view itself was enough to make any other kind of magic irrelevant.

The festival had lasted over a week. It was much written about in the British musical and countercultural press, and I believe that the festival is still being held annually, almost twenty years after our inaugural event with the great pyramid.

Chapter 25
Ireland

Driving back to London in a borrowed mini, wearing only light cotton shirts with the breeze whipping by, gave me a bad dose of flu. Somehow Scotch John and I ended up living with a bunch of students in a commune / residence / crash pad in Kingston. The flu was so bad I was knocked out for several days, and even had mild hallucinations. One day I woke up feeling better, and as I hadn't eaten for several days I wandered out into the streets of Kingston. I bought a carton of milk and wolfed it down.

I decided at that moment to hitchhike through Ireland, with fantasies of finding a croft cottage to use as a home base. I hitchhiked to Liverpool, where I met a seedy character on a back street who wanted to trade his leather shoes for my runners. I stumbled into the Liverpool ferry docks, and caught the all night ferry to Belfast. There were some Irish nursing students on the trip, and I stayed up all night flirting with them. One of them gave me her school address, and told me to look her up.

We docked in Belfast in early dawn light, and I stumbled off groggy from lack of sleep into the war torn streets. There were signs of the violence everywhere, although the shopkeeper in the little grocery where I bought some food was very friendly.

Belfast was no place for a longhaired pacifist, and quickly I hitched a ride with a respectable-looking young guy with short hair and a suit. As we were pulling into the outskirts of Belfast, we got stuck in traffic behind a lorry load of British troops. To torment us, they aimed their mounted machinegun at us. Perhaps we looked like a mismatched couple of guys, but my feeling was that they were doing it for enjoyment rather than for their protection.

The young businessman was only going as far as Armagh, the notorious border county which had been the scene of many IRA and counter IRA bombings and shootings. I was let out by a truck stop, and although it was early evening, I was exhausted from the ferry ride and the experiences of the war zone which is Belfast.

I crossed the road into the brush at the edge of the truck stop, and curled up to sleep about twenty feet from the road. As I was dozing off, I noticed a sinister omen next to me, the skeleton of a bat hanging from a bush. Despite the clinging bat skeleton, I fell into a sound sleep, only being awakened once when a truck motor started up. Then in the dead of the night a screaming howl woke me up with the shivers! It was like nothing I had ever heard. It was longer and louder than a human scream, more painful and mournful and dangerous. All I could think of was a Banshee! I quivered in my sleeping bag, not daring to move, and not feeling secure hidden in the bushes with the hanging bat. Thank God the scream didn't repeat, and I finally fell back asleep:

**Bat skeleton
hung on a shrub
banshee scream!**

The next day I got a lift to Sligo, which is on the west coast of Ireland. My lift took me into a pub in the small town, and got me quite drunk on just a couple of pints of real Irish Guinness. After saying goodbye to my benefactor, I wandered into the black night and fell asleep in a field. Minutes later the Guinness curdled, and I puked my guts out. I wasn't a pleasant sight to behold the next morning:

**Rocky Irish field
waking to the smell of
vomit and Guinness**

I began walking the narrow road - it was almost more of a cart trail - which was the main highway connecting Sligo with Galway. Past hilly little graveyards and quaint cottages beside trout streams. Mile after mile I walked for days, with only a car passing every couple of hours. In my deteriorating state, I didn't look like much of an attraction for good conversation to the few motorists, and so I walked four or five hours a day, and then slept besides the Sligo road at night.

Finally a car stopped for me. Two sexy Danish hitchhikers had insisted that the young Irish lad driving stop for me, and they drove me into Galway. The girls and I headed for the nearest pub, and had a pint. All the locals gathered round, and several of them performed their pub tricks. One played the flute, another sang, and one even danced for us. They were disappointed that we didn't have any special talents to show them, and they seemed sad that their exotic looking visitors weren't really very entertaining.

The girls and I headed for the outskirts of town, and I thought a very exciting evening was shaping up. Unfortunately every male hitchhiker for miles around had the same idea, and we all crowded into their little tent like good brothers and sisters of the road, and nobody got lucky.

The next morning we all started hitching. I got a lift on the back of a motorbike for five or six miles, but it turned out to be my next to last lift in Ireland. For days I walked the central road crossing back from Galway in the west to Dublin in the east. At night I slept in ditches, except once outside a town halfway to Dublin I slept in a tent with some local schoolboys.

I wandered on along the lonely highway. Althought it was a major road, there wasn't a lot of traffic. The few pounds I had started with had run out, and I hadn't eaten a full meal in weeks. Just as evening fell, I met a nice middle-aged lady who took me to her house and fed me dinner. I think it was some sort of retribution on her husband - I probably got to eat his dinner while he was in a pub. Luckily for me he didn't materialize, or my bones would probably be in an Irish graveyard.

I thanked her for the very welcome meal, and ambled to the outskirts of town to find my usual resting place in a ditch. I chose a spot several hundred yards from a deserted-looking house, and fell asleep with a full stomach. Around midnight I was awakened by the noises of a loud party from the house. For a moment I even thought of joining the wild goings-on, but I was so stuffed I fell back asleep.

When I next awoke it was dawn. I rubbed the sleep from my eyes, and peered through the thinning mist at the house where the rowdy party had taken place all night. It was deserted! No cars, no drunken bodies strewn on the lawn, nothing. The house was as deserted-looking as when I had first seen it the evening before. God knows what had transpired all night in the old house, or had it all been my imagination, the result of indigestion caused by my first real meal in weeks?

Chapter 26
Wales

I walked most of the winding road from Galway to Dublin. By now I looked like a real man of the road, to the extent that a gypsy family living in a caravan invited me for tea like a long lost uncle.

A businessman driving a van already loaded with hitchhikers picked me up, and drove me the final ten miles to Dublin. I found my way to the docks, and learning the departure time for the next ferry to Wales, I spent a few hours watching the lawn bowlers in a park.

When we landed in Wales, I was held for questioning by a police officer. I did look suspicious, or at least unusually dirty, even for a hippie. I asked why he was questioning me, and he made up a story about someone fitting my description skipping out on bed-sitters. It was just a pretext for questioning me, and when he was satisfied I was a harmless hippie wanderer, he pointed at the high wire fence surrounding the compound, and told me to go. Not wanting to hang around, I scrambled over the fence and into Anglesea, Wales.

And so began another trek. North Wales was a favourite with British vacationers, none of whom wanted a scruffy hippie for company in their already overloaded little cars. So I walked and walked, only getting two short rides in three days. The first night I met up with two students and shared their tent for the night.

The second night I slept in a field by a stream. As soon as I settled in for the night, it began to pour. Having no tent for shelter, I spent a miserable, soaked night. When I awoke early, the first thing I did was pluck the tick off my stomach, which had joined me for nourishment. After the terrible storm, the day broke fresh and clear. I had slept, or tried to sleep, in a beautiful country meadow, with a picturesque trout stream winding through. A man was flyfishing for his breakfast, and the world seemed bright and clear and alive again:

A tick for company
on my starving belly

My money and food had long run out, and I hadn't eaten anything for three days. Awakening in another field after my daily twenty mile hike, I got a lift from a sex-obsessed male driver, who wanted to know if, "all these hitchhikers need fucking or sucking or what?" As soon as we reached the next town, I bailed out, leaving the pervert driver to his fantasies.

I was literally starving. Two trendy young guys, with expensive hippie-style clothes and long but manicured hair, were hanging around the downtown area. Realizing only my pride was coming between starvation and food, I panhandled them for change. They gave me a few bob, about 50¢. I dragged myself into the local supermarket and bought the most nutritional food I could afford, a small jar of baby food. When I came back outside with my baby food, the students were still there. When they saw what I had bought, they took pity on me, and invited me to go back with them for a real meal.

James and Ron were university students working as waiters for the summer in a local hotel. They smuggled me a delicious meal of roast chicken, potatoes and gravy, and milk. It was the first solid meal I had had since the lady in the little Irish town had fed me over a week before. They put me up for the night in the room they shared in the old staff building, which had been the original coach house for the hotel. They were pleased to have a real travelling hippie for company, and lots of other students joined us in their room. James was a very accomplished guitar player, and we smoked dope and sang along with his playing until late into the night.

The night porter had just quit, and the next day I applied for the job. To my surprise the hotel manager gave me a trial job of cleaning up the kitchen, and I eagerly went to work scrubbing and polishing. I passed the test, and was made night porter. It was mid-August when I arrived in Llangollen. James and Ron delighted in showing me the sights of the famous town, which every year hosted an international music festival known as an Eisteddfod. Llangollen was ringed with hills so high that they were almost mountains, and the River Dee rushed through the centre of town under an old stone bridge. On our days off we would go swimming in the rapids above the bridge. Other days we trekked up Plas Newydd to the ruined Welsh fortress perched on the summit.

September arrived, and James and Ron departed for university. I stayed on, enjoying an Indian summer. I had become friends with some of the local lads, and often had a pint with them at one of the pubs before I started my all-night shift. A group of them were interested in rock music, and they were pleased to have a world-travelled hippie introduce them to the hippie lifestyle.

They all decided to try LSD, and so a bunch of us took the bus into Chester, an ancient city just inside the English border. A crumbling Roman wall still guarded the city's circumference. We managed to score some purple micro-dots from a nasty American dealer, who kept insisting that I swallow the whole handful of acid, a dose that would send anybody off the deep end.

Five or six of the locals camped the next night in the ruins of a monastery. I didn't want to drop acid, still feeling dislocated from all my travels. They had a great time, though, tripping all night in the haunted ruins, although one girl got so nervous she pooped in her pants.

The leaves were turning, and I spent the nights cleaning the old hotel, and the mornings wandering the rugged countryside. I also met Mary one night, a very horny eighteen-year-old who sometimes worked as a maid in the hotel. One night she stayed on after her duties, and we ended up necking in the library of the hotel. I hadn't had sex for months, and so I risked my job and took her back to my room in the coach house.

Chapter 27
The Rich Hippie

My brother Jeremy visited me in the early summer of 1972. We retraced part of my earlier trip to Ireland, and after returning to Britain by ferry we stayed overnight at a bed and breakfast in Anglesea to clean up. Then we began hitching south to visit Devon and Cornwall, the beautiful southwestern counties.

Our ride took us past Stonehenge. The driver seemed very knowledgeable about the ancient druids, and he finally confessed that he was one himself. "You've both invited to attend the druid festival on the Stonehenge site on the night of the summer solstice," he told us. "There are still hundreds of practicing druids in Great Britain, and we gather around fires on a plain near Stonehenge for the solstice every summer. Druids come from all over, and both of you would be most welcome."

A few more rides and we reached Devon. For a few hours we didn't get any lifts, and we were content to roam down the quiet country roads, surrounded by fields and forests. As we passed through a hamlet, a police car suddenly pulled up beside us. He wanted to see our identification, and we pleaded that we had to go to the washroom. Inside the washroom of the closest garage, Jeremy flushed an ounce of hash he had been carrying in his shoe down the toilet. We returned to the police car, and after the officer made a cursory check of our passports, he bid us good luck with our hitching. All that dope down the drain for nothing.

We continued walking, and nothing eventful happened for several hours. A speeding Rolls Royce limousine sailed by, and then came to a stop and began backing up. "Hi, you guys need a lift?" A young long-haired guy with an American accent was the driver. We climbed aboard the luxury car, which must have been worth ten or twenty thousand pounds.

"I'm Thomas. Say, you guys don't know where I could score some hash, do you?" Thomas' benevolence had a practical side. He was a university student on vacation, and he was nervous about scoring dope. "The car puts a lot of heads off. They think I'm a narc," he explained.

Jeremy still had a little hash hidden somewhere, and he offered to share a smoke with Thomas. "Why don't you guys come back to my place, and we'll smoke it there? In fact I could use some company. Where are you guys from?"

We exchanged brief life histories. Thomas was from the northeastern U.S. His dad was a high ranking diplomat assigned to Great Britain, and Thomas was visiting for the summer. The Rolls whisked along the country lanes, almost bruising the hedgerows. We had to slow to ten miles an hour to negotiate the final drive to Thomas' 'house', which was a gorgeous mansion.

It was getting dark, and Thomas invited us into the huge house and fixed us some dinner. Then we retired to his room, where we lounged on the floor while Jeremy rolled a hash joint. Thomas even had a TV set in this remote country setting, and the programme was interrupted by a bulletin that George Wallace of Alabama had been shot. We were stunned, and then we cheered. Wallace was one of the most notorious racists in the American South, and his shooting seemed an omen of the changing times.

We resumed getting stoned, and Thomas told us more about his life. He had won a Rhodes scholarship, but then he added, "Maybe it had something to do with my father, or my neighbourhood. Lots of kids from my neighbourhood won scholarships." When he got really high he began leafing through a catalogue of used Jaguars and Rolls Royces.

Thomas was a good host, despite his lack of grounding in reality. We were all longhaired brothers who smoked dope. It was just that some of us were richer than others. When we mentioned that we were planning on going to St. Ives, the legendary fishing village where Donovan had written many of his songs, Thomas volunteered to drive us there the next day.

We arrived in St. Ives in style. We made quite a hit, driving down the main street to the docks, where we said our farewells. Jeremy and I immediately began hunting for a place to doss for the night, and we soon met some hippies who were crashing in an old concrete bunker left over from World War II. The bunker was on the edge of St. Ives, and on top of the cliffs that led up from the village. Below us the Atlantic crashed into the rocks of the coast, while we spread our sleeping bags on the floor with about five or ten other dossers. In the flickering candlelight we could make out the graffiti carved or burned into the roof of the bunker, a history of the hundreds of dossers and men of the road before us who had slept in St. Ives on this spot. We searched for a message from Donovan among the scrawls and smoke writings of 'Dosser Dave from Newcastle' and the like.

The sun woke us early in our exposed position on the cliffs. Jeremy and I found some wild leeks, and cooked them up with eggs in our skillet, which we shared with the others. Early morning in St. Ives, with the sun shining over the sea and the day at our feet. A different style of castle from our lodging of the night before, but no less satisfying:

Leeks and eggs
smoke drifting over
Cornish cliffs

Chapter 28
Mescaline On The Barbican

Jeremy's vacation time was up, and he returned to Miami. I stayed on with a gang of hippies we had met in Plymouth, having nowhere else to go. Shortly after I settled in Plymouth a festival was held on the island in Plymouth Harbour. I went on the ferry with John, Simon and Brian Blood. It was a short and pleasant ride over, although the bay was choppy. The island was hilly, and the festival site was on a level plateau at the top of the island. Local bands were playing, and movies were being shown in some caves. Simon scored some mescaline, and we both took a tab.

Mescaline is generally a softer trip than LSD, without as much of an edge, although equally as hallucinatory. We sat in the caves for a while, and then as the mescaline began to take effect, we roamed above ground to the festival site. The fluttering banners and the music and the colourful hippies were overwhelming, so Simon and I decided to explore the island.

The mescaline was making us bouncy, and we scrambled around the rockface of the island enjoying the beautiful scenery. We didn't realize just how adventurous the trip had made us, until we looked down the steep rock cliffs and saw a troop of boy scouts practicing rock climbing far below us!

At nightfall we took the ferry back to the mainland, where we docked on the Barbican, the notorious old sailors' hangout. To relax from our trip, we went into one of the sailors' haunts, and got loaded on cheap draft beer. Drinking is an ideal way to come down from a psychedelic trip. The booze eases paranoia, and eventually makes sleeping possible.

The bar's habitués gave us a few stares, but they had seen far stranger sights in their lives than a group of longhaired kids acting stoned. The after-effects of the mescaline combined with the draft gave us a warm and glowing feeling, and somehow we made it back up the hilly backstreets of Plymouth to our flat.

Acid in our tea
we get drunk in a pub
with fishermen

GLOSSARY

acid: LSD

acid trip: to experience LSD

aggro: skinhead violence

au pair girl: a domestic worker from a foreign country

bedsitter: a rental room, esp. in a private house, usually rented by a student

Bobby: British cop

bummer: bad acid trip; bad experience in general

cannabis: marijuana/hashish

chapbook: short collection of poetry, often self-published

chillum: a small pipe for smoking hashish

crash: sleep

crash pad: a place to sleep

dharma: "the way" in Buddhism

dossers/dossing: people who sleep outdoors, or anywhere they have to

freak: a hippie; a head

freak out: to have a bad acid trip; to get very upset

ganger: a lead work hand; foreman

greaser: a biker

groover: weekend hippie; trendy poseur

haibun: prose interspersed with haiku (e.g. this book)

haiku: short, imagistic, insightful pieces of poetry

hash/hashish: cannabis resin (highly concentrated marijuana)

head: an experimenter with psychedelic drugs; a hippie

I Ching: "the book of changes"; a guidebook for creating and interpreting patterns to assist in making important decisions

joint: hey, you know what this is! - a marijuana cigarette

ley line: sacred lines which cross the planet, carrying spiritual energy

love-in: a gathering of hippies/flower children

mod: "modern boy"; stylish youth from the early1960s UK

narc: narcotics cop; also to inform on someone

nicked: arrested

nosh: to eat

NSU: non-specific uritis: a social disease

Paki bashing: racist attacks on people of colour

pensione: small rental rooming house in Spain

power tripper: authoritarian personality type

psychedelic/psychedelia: coined by Timothy Leary to describe a blissful state achieved by taking drugs like LSD; hallucinogenics

purple micro-dot: a strong tablet of LSD

rocker: greaser; biker

Scouse: a person from Liverpool; Liverpuddlian accent

scrumpy: strong cider

skinhead: a shaved head racist, usually from the lower class

squat: an abandoned building which becomes occupied by homeless people; a crash pad

STP: very strong hallucinogenic drug

straight: non drug user; a Muggle to Harry Potter fans

Teddy boy: an Elvis Presley wannabe in 1950s England

toke: to smoke hash/pot/marijuana/weed/grass/charge

tor: hollow sacred hill

trendy: a pretentious person or poseur; a fake hippie

The following is a brief memoir by another Eel Pie Island communard. It was written by "Prophet Chris" mentioned in chapter 8, "More Eel Piers". Weed became his legal name several decades ago, and this piece was first posted on his excellent website. "OJ" is the shorter nickname of Oddjob, the Australian biker mentioned in the same chapter. Many thanks to Weed for letting us include his parallel memories.

Met OJ on Eel Pie '69

First came across OJ in '69 on Eel Pie Island, which lies about half way between Richmond and Kingston, some 12 miles south-west of central London. An interesting place with a long history, it's rumoured to have once been the site of a monastery and much later to have been used as a courting ground (or more likely a scene of seduction) by Henry VIII. About 35 of us were living in the recently abandoned, somewhat derelict but still beautiful 3-storey hotel with its extravagant balcony looking out across the river towards Ham House and Petersham Meadows. There were various outhouses, and a large adjacent building said to have been the first in England to have an interior sprung dance-floor when it opened around the turn of the century.

Living on what is the largest island in the Thames, with only a narrow gently arching foot-bridge connecting it to the Twickenham side of the river, it was easy to fall under its spell and imagine that this was indeed a place where magic and fantasy lingered. The island is perhaps 1/3 of a mile long and not more than 100 yards across with small wooded areas at either end which had been left as bird sanctuaries. A winding path ran from the simple yet elegant bridge between a few small cottages down to the hotel and there split in two, one part going left to a boatyard and the other twisting right, through the hotel grounds and down to the water's edge.

I'd been to Eel Pie before, a few years earlier when it was still a thriving commercial venue - the hotel was run as a public

house by Jack Marr and sold "Newcastle Brown", an ale of
fearsome repute. The dancehall, reopened as a trad jazz club in
the 50s by Arthur Chisnell, had since become one of the main
centres of British rhythm'n'blues, having played host to the
likes of Alexis Korner, Cyril Davies and The Rolling Stones.
(Not that I went there often being more into acoustic folk-
blues, hitching down from Leeds to spend my weekends at Les
Cousins in Greek Street, attending the hallowed all-night
sessions of such as Bert Jansch, John Renbourn, Davy
Graham, Al Stewart, Mox, Jackson C Frank, Wizz Jones and
others.)

Anyway time flowed, and the place closed down, being left
empty for a couple of years until in 1969 a local arts group
managed to persuade the owner to rent out the now unused
hotel and dance-hall, the former as a place for various local
artisans to perform their crafts and the latter as a music and
theatre rehearsal space.

I bumped into Neil one afternoon on the sunny outdoor
terrace of the L'Auberge, that amazing cafe at the foot of
Richmond Hill whose fame had spread throughout the country
as a meeting place for those with nowhere to go. (Its reputation
was already firmly established by the time Andy and Maria
took it over. It continued to prosper, not only as a result of
the long hours of hard work that were put in, but also because
of a typically continental approach which combined firm
control with great tolerance. It was said that the police had
tried unsuccessfully on more than one occasion to close the
place down. Fortunately Andy was a member of the local
Watch Committee, or so the rumours went.) I was whiling away
my time awaiting customers for whatever it was that I might
have been selling, vaguely wondering where I was going to
sleep that night. Several of us had been of no fixed abode
since The China Tea Steam Navigation Company which was
moored further up the river had caught fire. Though not too

badly damaged, Captain Mike was now repelling all boarders. (The China Tea must have had more owners than any other boat on the river. It was bought by Queer Paul shortly afterwards, who'd borrowed the money from Canadian Chris, and a few months later it ended up being berthed and eventually grounded on the far side of the Hotel).

I'd been doing some work for the weird and wonderful cybernetics guru Gordon Pask (who not so long after became one of the few people in England to be connected to ARPAnet, and who, unknown to me at the time, had previously been involved with Arthur in Eel Pie jinks). Maybe this seemed sufficient reason for Neil to invite me to take on the role of secretary for the Richmond Arts Fellowship, the group negotiating the rental of the Eel Pie properties. So I asked about the chances of being able to stay there. He thought for a moment, as if the question were hypothetical, and said possibly, yes. So I said ok.

By this time the hotel was in the process of being moved into by a small group of unaffiliated anarchists who had returned to the area after an unsuccessful back to nature escapade the previous year. I'm not sure of the details, but it had been up towards the Scottish border – Cumberland, I think. Yes, Cliff mentions that period in his book *The Education of Desire*: "We were there for a year when we hit winter..." – I remember either him or Brennan talking about periods of great hunger, and how difficult it was to get a chicken to stay still when you're trying to decapitate it with an axe. Sounded grim, especially for the chickens.

Having now got the taste for communal living, but still battling against a phobia of the countryside, they decided on another attempt – it sort of goes against the grain to have an anarchist revolution without communes – but this time a bit closer to the dustbins of capitalism, from whence in an emergency sustenance might be salvaged. I think Cliff had an image of it being a centre of armed rebellion against the state – this was after all a period of activity by the Angry Brigade (England's answer to the Weathermen, or the Weather Underground as they later became). But support was lukewarm - in the end, the only guns seen were those produced 18 months later by some East End gangsters, brought in to ensure the dance-hall's peaceful transition of authority from the patronage of a nearby Hells Angels chapter to that of a slightly more professional management. Oh, and Polish Paul's water pistol, with which he attempted to hold up the local post-office. He was duly whisked off for 6 months under a section order... causing the older and wiser ones to nod their heads and mutter sagely "Could'afuckin'toldyerman, guns'r bad karma".

It would only have been a matter of time – minutes probably – before some of the locals turned up: "Hiya... heard you were moving in...", "Wow! this is really far out...", "Have you got any dope?", "Was this someone's room? aw sorry, man... is it all right if I just crash here for a while?". Within days the centre of Richmond and Twickenham's drug culture had moved from numerous minor scenes and recoalesced on Eel Pie Island, in the process collecting a wide variety of waifs and strays.

I'd set off myself, to visit Seamus who was already ensconced there. We'd known each other a few months. He'd come up from St Ives at the end of the previous summer. I'd been in the back room of the L'Auberge one evening, waiting for somebody to put some money in the jukebox, and overheard him talking about going to visit his friend Tats in South London. The name was familiar, and we started chatting and it turned out it was the same Tats who'd been in a house I'd stayed at for a while in East Dulwich, so I was able to pass on the warning to take care if he did go, 'cause the place had just been busted.' Out of such things friendships are made. Seamus had been sleeping under one of the nearby Railway Arches but decided it was more comfortable moving into this overcrowded rented room I'd inherited for a while – probably a close decision. Anyway we kept in touch – still do. But didn't succeed in seeing him that time. Got stopped, searched and arrrested for possession of drugs whilst crossing Richmond Bridge.

That was a comedy of errors! Sunny golden Autumn afternoon, clear blue sky, light breeze, me as always amazed at the gorgeous view of woods and meadows looking south along the river towards Petersham Fields, and generally feeling pretty good. "D'you want some acid?", said Roy, who was always very cool, swallowing a blotter. "Ok", said I. But it was not to be, for at this point the police interfered in the form of Dudley and his sidekick, the rather nasty members of the local drug squad. Not that I was too worried. As it all started happening, rather than throwing an incriminating matchbox into the river, I'd done my usual and pushed it into the torn lining of my jacket - it was only a couple of dex 10s. So they searched Roy and found nothing (cause he'd palmed it), and then they went through my pockets, and pulled out various stuff, and said: "What's this?"

Now generally I'm pretty lucky in these sort of situations, once being thoroughly shaken down while standing there with a large joint in my hand; another time throwing a bit of blow as the squad car skidded to a halt. They knew I'd just scored, they'd seen me drop it, so where was it? Or had I really just been trying to wind them up by pretending to throw something, and was still carrying? It wasn't 'till they drove off that I realised why they'd not found anything - one of the wheels had stopped directly on top of the dope, leaving it a bit squashed, but otherwise ok. (The very young Annabella, for whom it was destined, and on whom it was found when she was searched that evening on returning to Stanley Royds, the local mental hospital, never did admit who she'd got it from, though the police had been following her movements all day and knew practically everyone she'd had contact with. Fending off enquiries by angry psychiatrists able to threaten you with whatever they can rustle up from their store of mentally and physically disabling pharmaceuticals demands a rare courage. There are no awards for such heroism.) And then there was the time they'd tried to plant me, and all my pockets had holes in them...

But this time I'd fucked up... "Matches" said I. Wrong. I'd pushed the other box into my lining and left the pills in my pocket. Great!

So they searched Roy again, this time with much more attention and found the hit of acid; what should have been my hit of acid. And the pair of us got hauled off to Richmond cop shop, there to be interrogated in greater depth, 'coz they'd been watching me, and were damn sure that there was more to be found – kept threatening to break my guitar open, but finally decided they weren't getting anywhere. Until one of them idly picked up my jacket and casually flung it over the back of a nearby chair. And wouldn't you know, as it landed, the bottom of the jacket swung up against the chair and there was the smallest of rattles – the two drug squad guys looked at each other and dived for the jacket, ripped open the lining, grabbed the other matchbox, and spent the next 5 minutes examining its contents – 40 matches... Only as an afterthought did one of them take the jacket and give it a final couple of rips, just to make sure. And that was when the tubes of Centramina (Spanish amphetamines) fell out, tumbling all over the floor.

It was a bit rough, but mainly bluff, only a couple of blows and kicks from Dudley, who had a bit of a reputation for beating people up once he'd got them alone in the cells. He put on something of a performance, producing a bit of cannabis he claimed to have found and threatening to use it to bust the house of a friend I'd stayed at, before clumsily pretending to flush it down the toilet as a show of reasonableness. Being NFA meant no bail for me, and on top of that I was feeling bad about causing all this hassle for Roy. I apologised later, told him I'd wondered if he'd been all right. He said he'd been ok - the trip hadn't started coming on until he was in the cells, and anyway, they'd let him out after 4 or 5 hours. Very cool.

But I digress. So I moved into the two small rooms above the stage at one end of the dance-hall together with a few others who were floating between realities. Once a week the Arts Group would meet and discuss how to make some money for the rent. They decided to have a dance to raise some cash, with Mark Newton, a friend of a friend being brought in to run it. Except he turned up wearing shades, holding on to the leads of a couple of large alsations and generally behaving like a slick promoter. By the time he'd taken over the dance-hall for himself, Cliff and Jonathon had also managed to come to a rent agreement of £20 a week on behalf of those in the hotel, and the Arts Group found itself squeezed out, returning no doubt sadder but wiser to their original meeting-space. But who knows, without them...

One wondered why Michael Snapper, the owner, was prepared to become embroiled with such potentially inconvenient people. Well it turned out he owned most of the island. He'd also recently been refused permission by the planning authority to knock down the hotel in order to build potentially profitable flats and maisonettes. And maybe he assumed that it would just be a matter of time before the council realised that the only way to get rid of the unwashed hordes that had descended on the place was to have it demolished. I suspect that as well as being a successful local businessman, he was something of a bohemian and still retained more than a streak of libertarian humour.

I continued living above the stage for a while in return for performing occasional menial duties at the dances put on by Mark with the assistance of Scotch Dougie. Some good bands played there, the most memorable being Stray, The Edgar Broughton Band (they really got the audience going with their Out Demons Out anthem, nice guys – generous with their dope), and Hawkwind (though then they were called Hawkwind Zoo – the name change came about a month later... they performed in complete darkness with just the red LEDs of their amps shining – a part of the evening remains particularly clear to me, mainly because I was tripping quite heavily about three feet above their heads, and I can still remember the vibrating floorboards... saw them again a few months ago as it happens, meeting up with my son Sol and some friends at a techno allnighter, but this time on E and a few shrooms – plus ça change).

After a couple of months I drifted into the hotel, which had become an acceptably out of control international crash-pad, many people arriving there via BIT. A year later the numbers had risen to 130 and still not stabilised. Various attempts were made to give it at least a name, if not a constitution. The words "Arts Lab" and "Commune" were bandied about by some, but never really caught on within the place. The excesses of the social anarchy which flourished there attracted amongst other things a constant stream of visitors (mainly to buy drugs), occasional media attention (local and national), and several invasions from gangs of skinheads and other adolescent tribes that inhabited the area. All the things that happened there, the good, the bad, and the strange – well, they're ten thousand stories in their own right.

OJ turned up pretty early on in all this. I think he'd been at the Arts Lab in Drury Lane and then been involved with the infamous squat at 144 Piccadilly when police stormed the building trying to retake it from the occupants. Hardly the

Easter Rising, but it's still remembered in UK underground culture as one of the great battles of the '60s. Part of the diaspora and still wearing his colours, OJ homed in on the Island effortlessly and cheerfully started getting a room together, rebuilding the second floor of one of the out-houses.

– Weed (June 1996)

Califonia Jon and Terry – Twickenham

Debbie and Canadian Chris
– Isabella Plantation, Richmond Park

Canadian Chris and Australian Danny

Group Wedding

Jumbo – Helle – Inga – Prophet Chris

Cornish John

Canadian Chris embarking – China Tea Steam Navigation

California Jon and Terry – L'Auberge Cafe

Wedding Afetrmath

Canadian Chris and Marion by the River Thames

About the Author

Eric Amann, publisher of *Haiku* magazine, gave Chris early encouragement circa 1967. Chris has been writing and publishing haiku his entire adult life. His work has consistently been at the forefront in the development of English language haiku and haibun, and the online version of this book is likely the most widely read English language haibun.

His poetry has been widely published internationally in literary magazines, anthologies and scholarly texts and broadcast on radio and TV. *EPID* has become a frequent reference for documentaries and historical books.

Chris is also known for lyrical and political poetry. In 1987 he was honoured with the inaugural Milton Acorn People's Poet Award. Chris has been active as an organizer of poetry events and associations. He founded Unfinished Monument Press in 1978, and the Main Street Library Poetry Series in Toronto in 1979. In 2007 he began coordinating annual Purdy Country Literary Festivals (PurdyFests). Chris was a founding member of Haiku Canada and the Canadian Poetry Association. He is an honourary life member of the Canada-Cuba Literary Alliance.

In 1989 he moved to an Ontario village on the edge of the Canadian Shield, where he earned his living as village librarian. Now retired, he wanders remote trails and acts as steward of his ZenRiver Gardens retreat. Chris' 2008 Hidden Brook Press collection, *ZenRiver: Poems & Haibun*, relates some of his experiences in this wild and untamed countryside. He continues to develop and promote this new subgenre of "shaman haibun" which he helped create with *ZR:P&H*. You can follow his poetry and activities on his blog *Riffs and Ripples from ZenRiver Gardens*.

Previous Collections by Chris Faiers

ZenRiver: Poems & Haibun (Hidden Brook Press, 2008)

Small Press Lynx (co-editor with Mark McCawley; co-published
 Unfinished Monument Press, Greensleeve Editions, 1991)

Eel Pie Dharma: a memoir/haibun (Unfinished Monument Press, 1990)

Moon City (haiku - Greensleeve Publishing, 1989)

13 Bohemian Dreams (Unfinished Monument Press, 1988)

Mr Library Man (Haiku Canada broadsheet, 1988)

Foot Through the Ceiling (Aya/Mercury Press, 1986)

5 Minutes Ago They Dropped The Bomb (Unfinished Monument Press, 1984)

The Unfinished Anthology (co-editor, Unfinished Monument Press, 1984)

Island Women (HMS Press, 1983)

White Rasta in Wintertime (Unfinished Monument Press, 1982)

Unacknowledged Legislator (blewointmentpress, 1981)

Sleeping in Ruins (haiku - Unfinished Monument Press, 1981)

White Rasta (Unfinished Monument Press, 1980)

College Streetcar Runs All Night (Unfinished Monument Press, 1979)

Dominion Day in Jail (Unfinished Monument Press, 1978)

Guest in a Garden (haiku - C&C Printing, 1969)

Cricket Formations (haiku - C&C Printing, 1969)

Credits

Haibun

This book was first published by Unfinished Monument Press in 1990 in Toronto under the title *Eel Pie Dharma*.

Webmaster Weed kindly posted *Eel Pie Dharma* online in the early 2000s, where it has been enjoyed by tens of thousands of readers.

The "Lavenham" chapter was published in *Haiku Canada Review*, Vol 3, Number 1, Feb. 2008

Haiku

The haiku have been widely individually published since the mid-1960s, including the magazines *Haiku, Haiku West, Haiku Highlights, Southwind, Janus SCTH, Inkstone, Origins, Wee Giant* and elsewhere.

They have also appeared in the anthologies *Canadian Haiku Anthology*, Three Trees Press, 1979, *Canadian Haiku Anthology*, Editions Asticou, 1985, *The Haiku Handbook*, McGraw Hill, 1985, *Synesthesia in Haiku* 1990, *A Magical Clockwork*, 1990, *The Modern English Haiku*, 1981, *Feast of Equinox*, 2007 and in many Haiku Canada Members' Anthologies, including the holographic anthologies.

Used as Source

BBC Radio 4 documentary 2007

Eel Pie Dharma was a source and inspiration for novelist Hari Kunzru for *My Revolutions* 2008, Dutton;

Eel Pie Island, Dan Van Der Vat and Michele Whitby, eds.Frances Lincoln Ltd., 2009

Won't Get Fooled Again: The Who from Lifehouse to Quadrophenia, Richie Unterberger, Jawbone Press, 2011

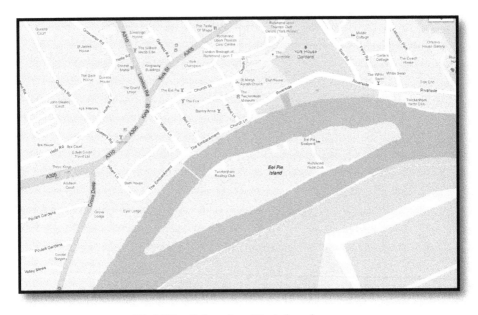

Eel Pie Island – Twickenham

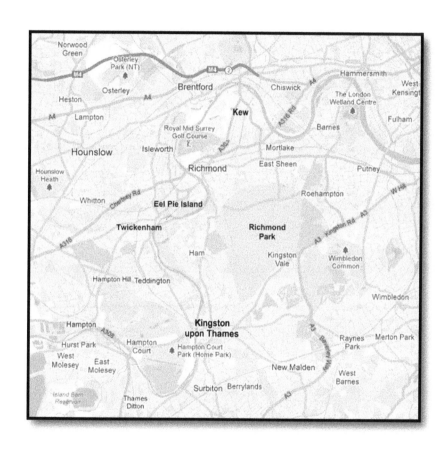

The Thames West London

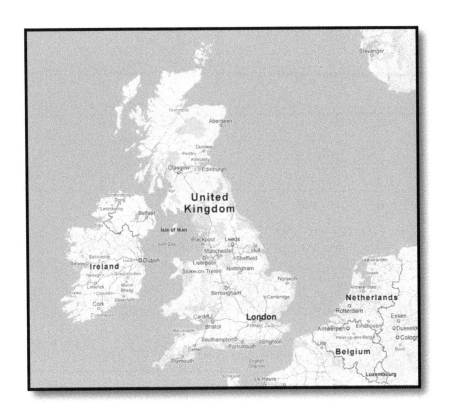

British Isles

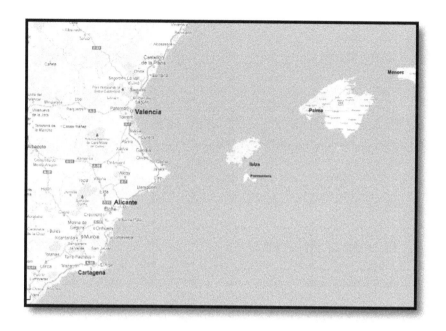

Formentera Island – Spain

Books in the North Shore Series

Find full information at
– http://www.HiddenBrookPress.com/b-NShore.html

Anthologies

Changing Ways is a book of prose by Cobourg area authors
including: Jean Edgar Benitz, Patricia Calder, Fran O'Hara
Campbell, Leonard D'Agostino, Shane Joseph, Brian Mullally.
Editor: Jacob Hogeterp – Prose – ISBN – 978-1-897475-22-5

That Not Forgotten - Editor – Bruce Kauffman with 118 authors
    – Prose and Poetry – ISBN – 978-1-897475-89-8

First set of five books

— **M.E. Csamer** – Kingston – *A Month Without Snow*
    – Prose – ISBN – 978-1-897475-87-2
— **Elizabeth Greene** – Kingston – *The Iron Shoes*
    – Poetry – ISBN – 978-1-897475-76-6
— **Richard Grove** – Brighton – *A Family Reunion*
    – Prose – ISBN – 978-1-897475-90-2
— **R.D. Roy** – Trenton – *A Pre emptive Kindness*
    – Prose – ISBN – 978-1-897475-80-3
— **Eric Winter** – Cobourg – *The Man In The Hat*
    – Poetry – ISBN – 978-1-897475-77-3

Second set of five books

— **Janet Richards** – Belleville – *Glass Skin*
    – Poetry – ISBN – 978-1-897475-01-0
— **R.D. Roy** – Trenton – *Three Cities*
    – Poetry – ISBN – 978-1-897475-96-4
— **Wayne Schlepp** – Cobourg – *The Darker Edges of the Sky*
    – Poetry – ISBN – 978-1-897475-99-5
— **Benjamin Sheedy** – Kingston – *A Centre in Which They Breed*
    – Poetry – ISBN – 978-1-897475-98-8
— **Patricia Stone** – Peterborough – *All Things Considered*
    – Prose – ISBN – 978-1-897475-04-1

Third set of five books

— **Mark Clement** – Cobourg – *Island In the Shadow*
  – Poetry – ISBN – 978-1-897475-08-9
— **Anthony Donnelly** – Brighton – *Fishbowl Fridays*
  – Prose – ISBN – 978-1-897475-02-7
— **Chris Faiers** – Marmora – *ZenRiver Poems & Haibun*
  – Poetry – ISBN – 978-1-897475-25-6
— **Shane Joseph** – Cobourg – *Fringe Dwellers* Second Edition
  – Prose – ISBN – 978-1-897475-44-7
— **Deborah Panko** – Cobourg – *Somewhat Elsewhere*
  – Poetry – ISBN – 978-1-897475-13-3

Forth set of five books

— **Diane Dawber** – Bath – *Driving, Braking and Getting out to Walk*
  – Poetry – ISBN – 978-1-897475-40-9
— **Patrick Gray** – Port Hope – *This Grace of Light*
  – Poetry – ISBN – 978-1-897475-34-8
— **John Pigeau** – Kingston – *The Nothing Waltz*
  – Prose – ISBN – 978-1-897475-37-9
— **Mike Johnston** – Cobourg – *Reflections Around the Sun*
  – Poetry – ISBN – 978-1-897475-38-6
— **Kathryn MacDonald** – Shannonville – *Calla & Édourd*
  – Prose – ISBN – 978-1-897475-39-3

Fifth set of three books

— **Tara Kainer** – Kingston – *When I Think On Your Lives*
  – Poetry– ISBN – 978-1-897475-68-3
— **Morgan Wade** – Kingston – *The Last Stoic*
  – Novel – ISBN – 978-1-897475-63-8
— **Kathryn MacDonald** – Shannonville – *A Breeze You Whisper*
  – Poetry – ISBN – 978-1-897475-66-9

Sixth set of three books

—**Bruce Kauffman** – *The Texture of Days, in Ash and Leaf*
  – Poetry – ISBN - 978-1-897475-86-7
— **Chris Faiers** – *Eel Pie Island Dharma: A hippie memoir/haibun*
  – A memoir in haibun form – ISBN - 978-1-897475-92-8
— **Theodore Michael Christou** – *an overbearing eye*
  – Poetry – ISBN – 978-1-897475-93-5